Henry Isham has taught seventh and eighth grade, analyzed financial statements, and assayed precious metals. He traveled a lot when he was younger and is now retired. Isham gardens and plays tennis as much as possible. When the COVID-19 shutdown loomed, he decided to pursue answers to a question which had interested him for some time.

Henry Isham

ILLINOIS 1000

AUSTIN MACAULEY PUBLISHERS™

LONDON • CAMBRIDGE • NEW YORK • SHARJAH

Ordering Information
Quantity sales: Special discounts are available on quantity purchases by corporations, associations, and others. For details, contact the publisher at the address below.

Publisher's Cataloging-in-Publication data
Isham, Henry
Illinois 1000

ISBN 9798886935042 (Paperback)
ISBN 9798886935066 (ePub e-book)
ISBN 9798886935059 (Audiobook)

Library of Congress Control Number: 2023919493

www.austinmacauley.com/us

First Published 2024
Austin Macauley Publishers LLC
40 Wall Street, 33rd Floor, Suite 3302
New York, NY 10005
USA

mail-usa@austinmacauley.com
+1 (646) 5125767

The figure on the cover is from George Catlin's painting, The Snow-Shoe Dance, used with permission of the Amon Carter Museum of American Art, Fort Worth, Texas.

George Catlin (1796-1872), The Snow-Shoe Dance, ca. 1875-78, lithograph with applied watercolor, Amon Carter Museum of American Art, Fort Worth, Texas, 2004.18.14

COUNTRIES
traversed by
MARQUETTE, HENNEPIN
and
LA SALLE.
GULF OF MEXICO
ARKANSAS
CENIS
Cadoes
Chicka
Natches Caroas Gumas
Red R.
R. Arkansas
R. Missouri
Quinipissas
Galveston Bay
Matagorda Bay
Mustang I.
Corpus Christi Bay
Rio Grande
Course of La Salle 1684
Cape San Antonio
Scale of Statute Miles

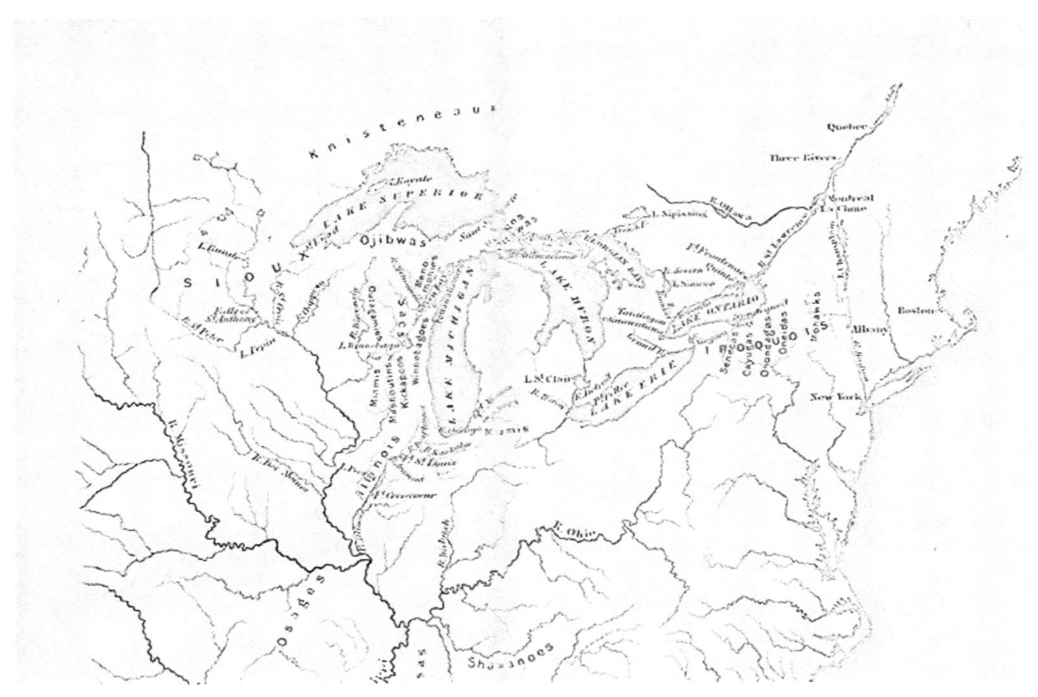

Knistenaux
Quebec
Three Rivers
Montreal
La Chine
R. Ottawa
L. Nipissing
R. St Lawrence
L. Isle Royale
LAKE SUPERIOR
SIOUX
Ojibwas
Sault Ste Marie
GEORGIAN BAY
L. Simcoe
Ft Frontenac
Bay of Quinte
L. Champlain
Boston
Fall of St Anthony
R. St Peter
L. Erie
Menomonies
Sacs
LAKE MICHIGAN
LAKE HURON
LAKE ONTARIO
Mohawks
Albany
Senecas
Cayugas
Onondagas
Oneidas
Miamis
Mascoutins
Kickapoos
Winnebagoes
L. St Clair
LAKE ERIE
New York
R. Missouri
R. Des Moines
ILLINOIS
R. Wabash
R. Ohio
Osages
Sas
Shawanoes

Introduction

Like most kids my generation, I spent considerable time pretending I was an Indian. I knew very little about them as everything I knew came from T.V. programs and the Thanksgiving pageant. As I grew older, I forgot about them or whoever it was who at some point in the distant past might have lived in the same Chicago suburb I did.

These ancient people came back to mind one night though, on a cab ride home from O'Hare Field.

The airport had been about to close due to an approaching blizzard, and I had had the good fortune to be placed with a couple headed to Lake Bluff, which was immediately north of my destination, Lake Forest. Our driver had a companion with him up front, which made a lot of sense in case we became stuck in a snowdrift and needed a push or help with a shovel. The cab grew dark as we left the terminal, the windows crusting over with snow. The only light came from the radio up front. Beside me in the darkness, the couple from Lake Bluff began a quiet but heated discussion. I tried to stay focused on the barely audible Mexican music coming over the radio.

Soon, we merged onto the toll road and began a steady 45 miles per hour on the nearly deserted highway. I could feel our driver relax. He had a sense of the road now and conditions were not getting any worse. He would drop me off first, he said to his friend softly, then the couple in Lake Bluff, and then they would head home, which turned out to be Highwood, just south of Lake Forest. My destination was one block east of Green Bay Road, the cabby continued. Green Bay Road, he explained to his friend, was the first road out of Chicago, an old military road that connected Chicago to Green Bay, Wisconsin. I had known that since I was a kid. A friend who lived almost next door had even found a small cannon ball in his yard which dated to when the road opened in the 1840s.

Then the cabby went further. Green Bay Road was very old. It went back before Columbus, all the way back to when the glaciers left, and the first people come onto the land.

January

Robert Lacy and Danny Danzinger in their wonderful book, The Year 1000, wrote about the English people in that year, and as I read of the English, their activities, their health, their beliefs, and other aspects of tenth-century English life, something brought me back to that cab ride.

"What," I wondered, "was life like for Indians living in Lake Forest in the year 1000?"

Lacey and Danzinger lament the scarcity of material available to them, noting that when Henry VIII closed England's monasteries, starting in 1532, his men burned almost all the manuscripts and records, nearly everything monks had ever written going back 500 years. Monks had acted as England's historians. Almost everything was lost[1].

Still, Lacey and Danzinger had some written material from the period to work with. Indians did not write, not as we know it.

The Julius Work Calendar is one of the few documents from a monastery to have survived. It dates to the year 1020. The manuscript's twelve illustrations, one for each month, show activities that English men, yeomen and nobles,

---

[1] Lacy and Danzinger

engaged in. Each illustration introduces different aspects of life in 10th-century England.

January's illustration is of two yeomen plowing a field with four oxen. One man leads the teams while the other guides the plow from behind. A third man is sowing seed into the furrows. Earth's temperature was several degrees warmer in 1000, a period known as the Little Optimum. Plowing might have occurred in England, though probably not in Scotland.

Temperatures cooled later. The 1600s is a period referred to as "The Little Ice Age," much colder than now. Wheat was more common than rye in 1000. Five hundred years later, during the reign of Henry VIII, it would be the reverse, rye being the more productive in the colder, damper weather. Henry and his court preferred the more costly wheat bread.

Another interpretation is that this illustration is symbolic. The twelfth scene of the Julius Work Calendar depicts activities that took place earlier in the year, and its harvest scene is said to symbolize closure. Similarly, the opening of the year might be shown as the sowing of seed into fresh furrows, an activity which may not have taken place until a few months later.

England, Scotland, and Wales together are 81,000 square miles. Across the Atlantic Ocean, starting at the ocean's edge and stretching westward for over a thousand miles, was the Eastern Woodland, 2,000,000 square miles of forest, mountain, swamp, and swift-flowing rivers.

The Indians who lived in Lake Forest did not have cattle or wheat, and they did not use metal tools, but, in the warmer weather of that period, they too may have been preparing the ground for planting. Early inhabitants of England used antlers to break the soil. The Indians probably did the same. They may have set fire to the prairie the previous fall and, in the spring, broken the ash-laden soil while it was still soft from melted snow. It is often thought that the Indians left nature undisturbed. It's not so. They also set the forests on fire from time to time to clear out undergrowth and encourage browse, which, in turn, increased the number of deer. Plains Indians lived on buffalo. To a lesser extent, Lake Forest's would have depended on the white-tailed deer.

Without draft animals or metal tools, the Indians broke the sod with implements of antler or wood or stone. They had none of the grains available to a European of that era, and they did not yet have either corn or beans. These last two of the "Three Sisters" had not yet been adapted to a climate as far north as Lake Forest's.

The Indians could have planted a variety of the first of the Three Sisters, pumpkin and squash[2]. To keep the different varieties from crossing, separated growing areas were required. The Indians would also have planted sunflower and its near relative, Jerusalem artichoke, which produces small tubers as well as seed.

The rest of what the Indians planted, and upon which some tribes spent most of their labor, we think of today as weeds. Farmers apply herbicides specifically formulated to kill off the very plants that sustained the Indians of North America for more than 9000 years.

---

[2] Anthology

Pigweed and lambsquarter were also consumed by Europeans but, by 1000, left mostly to their livestock. These related plants, as well as ragweed, knotweed, sump weed, and others which produce multitudes of tiny seeds, were grown as staples by the Indian tribes of the Upper Midwest. For much of the year, cattails or tubers of Jerusalem artichoke might have been their most available carbohydrate. Humans can live healthy lives without them, but carbohydrates increase the amount of edible calories available to a society where animal protein and fat is limited. Introduction of the potato from South America contributed to a tripling of Europe's population within two generations. Before that, for thousands of years, grains such as wheat, rye, barley, and oats had been the best source for these calories.

Until Indians acquired corn which could mature between frosts at northern latitudes, they would have spent less time in their fields than their English counterparts and more time scavenging and hunting. They would have needed to.

A period more closely corresponding in England to that of the Indians of Lake Forest in 1000 would have been about 4000 B.C. Northwest Europe was still a society of hunter-gathers with almost no agriculture. Around 7000 B.C., the English Channel filled in, and England/Wales/Scotland became an island. Where people had lived was now the North Sea. Then around 4000 B.C., from today's Middle East, came new tribes with seeds and animals.

The domesticated cattle of these newcomers acted as weapons of mass destruction. Smallpox and measles entered the human sphere through our ancestors' close association with cattle. As these newcomers progressed into Europe, the pre-existing populations fell away quickly as these diseases and others spread from Portugal to Finland. Over many generations, the survivors came to have the same degree of partial immunity as the newcomers. They adapted to the use of crops and domesticated animals and merged with them.

The Indians developed plants they found in the Southeast of the United States into many varieties of squash and pumpkin, perhaps as early as 2000 B.C. By 1000, Indians in Lake Forest were eating wild beans but did not yet have good crop seed. They most likely would have known of corn. They may even have been eating corn meal and trying to grow it themselves, but not yet succeeding in getting a viable crop.

Corn is thought to be a cross of two varieties of grass. The hybrid was improved over many centuries before it became a staple for the Indians of Central America.

Slowly, corn was developed to be more cold-hardy and to mature during shorter and shorter growing seasons as it moved north along the Gulf of Mexico and then up the Mississippi River, north past Cahokia, Illinois, and east up the Ohio River Valley, and from there into Canada by the early 1600s.

As well as food crops, Indians grew bottle gourds for carrying water and for material they needed to keep dry. Genetic analysis indicates that the bottle gourd was developed in Asia and came to America with the earliest Americans around 16,000 B.C. The small number of people who crossed from Asia, who may have needed years to complete a crossing through Beringia, brought with them seeds which could only be used if and when they again arrived at an anticipated warmer climate. They brought bottle gourd seeds but apparently no others.

These earliest Americans also brought dogs with them. Indian dogs descended entirely from Eurasian wolves and not at all from the North American wolf. At the time of crossing, the dogs were already separated into three breeds: work dogs, dogs raised for their hair, and a third for eating. The Indians never bred shepherding or herding dogs as they had no flocks. They did not breed dogs like mastiffs for defense against wolves. Canis lupus lupus, the European wolf, the progenitor of the dog, was known to attack humans. Packs of them terrorized Paris during the winter of 1450. But Canis lupus lycaon, the North American wolf, was different. It attacked pumas, moose, and bears, but, seemingly, not humans.

A crop grown in the New World as far back as any, except for the bottle gourd, was tobacco.

Smoking tobacco was universal among the North American tribes. Tribes who planted nothing else planted tobacco. Over forty varieties were developed. Trade was widespread, some varieties traveling halfway across the country.

The tribe in Lake Forest would have spent most of January inside long houses. Long houses were built by planting saplings in two rows, bending them in arcs and tying them down, and then covering them with rolls of bark. A line of firepits ran down the middle. Above each pit was an opening for light to enter and smoke to escape. Long houses were crowded, smoky, and with fleas and lice. English households were like that too. The English hung meat from their ceilings to cure in the smoke of their fires. The Indians probably did the same. One great difference was that while the Indians of Lake Forest never lacked for fuel, for their English counterparts, wood was always in short supply. Winters were cold, and wool was essential.

Mid-winter was not often a time of true hunger for the English yeomen, with their stores of grain. It was different for the Indians. Pumpkins take up space. Collecting small seeds is labor-intensive.

While cold was a winter constant for the English yeomen, for the Indians, the winter constant would have been hunger. A hoped-for event was a heavy snowfall. George Catlin's famous painting, The Snowshoe Dance, is of Indians preparing for a winter hunt. Snow is falling. Yet, the dancing men are nearly naked. The men are pre-gaming, psyching up, praying. The dance started at night so they could head off at first light or as soon as the storm passed. They wear snowshoes. Snow in Lake Forest is never powdery. It is always dense and packs down. With a heavy snowfall, the Indians held an advantage over the deer. The deer needed to extricate each foot over and over as they ran. The men on their snowshoes sank down hardly at all.

They may have headed to a meadow not far away, which the men avoided most of the year and where over the summer and fall and on the eve of the storm, the women had left salt.

The men approach silently, smelling the air and checking for any shift in wind direction, keeping their dogs quiet and in check. They may have had a variety of strategies, hoping to catch the herd still half-asleep after the storm, waiting for the sun to warm them. Then the men would chase the deer toward a gauntlet or down a ravine onto a beach or out into a marsh. They would have used spears with atlatls, a weapon their ancestors had used on deer for eons. Some of the men might have used the recently reintroduced bow and arrow. If the kill was adequate, the Indians would not have the dogs drag whole carcasses back to camp but would fieldstrip the deer and reward the dogs with the innards, saving the organs whose healing properties were long known.

When the French arrived in Canada in the 1500s, some of the Indians farmed. Others still lived as hunter-gathers. At the start of each winter, the Algonquins, hunter-gathers, disbursed into the forest in small bands as larger groups would not find enough game to survive a winter. Winters were hard on the hunter-gatherers. Many did not reappear after one particularly harsh winter.

In 1646, a Jesuit priest and a young boy accompanied a band of Hurons traveling from Montreal back to their village near Lake Huron. The young boy was to live with the Hurons and be brought up by them so that he might later act as an ambassador and translator. The boy was probably an orphan taken in and raised by the order, and their strongest candidate. The journey took 17 days and involved over forty portages. Rations were two meals a day of a small portion of ground corn mixed with water. No fires were lit for fear of the Iroquois. They slept on the ground at night without cover.

The boy nearly died. The priest paid for more food for the boy, some of the Hurons giving up their own. The ability of Indians to survive on short rations was frequently commented on by the French.

At other times, Indians ate heartily. Rather than offend a host, an Indian might eat until he died.

A colony of French escaped death at the hands of the Iroquois when an ally induced the tribe to feast for him to undo a curse which had been placed upon him. He induced his guests to eat to the point of extreme distress, and then the French made their escape[3].

By the 1600s, most of the tribes in the upper Midwest and Northeast grew corn and beans and lived in established settlements. In 1000, Indians in Lake Forest would have been less settled, moving more often, timing their arrivals to those of migrating birds and fish and the maturities of edible plants.

Acorns may have been looked on the same way on both sides of the Atlantic, food eaten only during times of scarcity. The English let their hogs eat the acorns and then ate the hogs. With no competition from hogs, bears were more prevalent in North America than they ever were in England. Bears or hogs killed in late fall after months of consuming acorns, fungi, and grubs represented a lot of quality fat and meat. Bears had large pelts, and their fat had many uses. The black bears around Lake Forest were smaller than the grizzly bears which lived further to the west. Still, they were dangerous and best left alone until they had started hibernation and then located with dogs. Bears cleared the forest of dead animals, turned the earth in search of grubs, and spread berries far and wide. Like hogs, bears carry trichinosis, and their meat must be cooked thoroughly.

---

[3] Francis Parkman

For much of the year, squirrels might be snared and the acorns harvested in that way as well. Or, the acorns may have been gathered and prepared into a bread as Indians in California did. Those tribes increased their harvests by selectively cutting away trees which were not oaks.

Europeans described Indian dogs as wolf-like, bred for hunting and hauling, with others bred for their hair or to be eaten. Dog feasts were special occasions. Dog hair was spun and woven into cloth. It's strange, but while genetic analysis indicates that it is possible as few as fifty individuals may have crossed over Beringia to populate the New World, they brought along with them three separate breeds of dog.

In tenth-century England, a man's diet depended on his place in the social order, but whether he was a noble or a slave, his bones and teeth were well formed. Warfare in England at this time was almost constant, but waged, for the most part, after the harvest was in. The yeoman was less likely to starve over a bad winter than his Indian counterpart, but if his oxen became ill or a frost came too early or too late, it could mean ruin.

The iron wheeled plow had been used in England for perhaps 1000 years. Oxen were preferred to horses. They cost less to keep and had fewer health problems. Also, harnesses which made effective use of a horse's strength, the front legs, had only recently been introduced. The seven centuries of near-constant war that followed the Romans' departure had put England's animal husbandry into decline. The yeomen's oxen were much smaller than ones the Romans would have used. As far back as any yeoman could have known, in the spring, yeomen planted, birds flew north, and trees leafed out. It was an unquestioned activity. Yeomen planted every spring.

The Indians in Catlin's painting dance nearly naked in midwinter at night, inured to cold as well as to hunger and insects. Days were short. They were shorter everywhere in England as all of England lies north of Lake Forest. Their worlds were not very much alike.

February

In February's illustration of the Julius Work Calendar, two yeomen are trimming grape vines. Vines were trimmed in February when they were most dormant. The Romans had grown grapes in England during their occupation, and winemaking may have preceded them to the island by as much as 1000 years. Vineyards were well established and maintaining vines was a valued skill among those who lived in or nearby the monasteries, abbeys, and other religious settlements in tenth-century England. In that warmer period vines grew as far as seventy miles north of London. A lot of acreage could have been devoted to them. The wine ran about 4% alcohol. Mixed half and half with water, it killed most bacteria.

No grapes worth picking grew in North America. (The Concord grape is half-European in its ancestry).

Beer was the common beverage in England. It was flavored with many different herbs: hops but also with wormwood and horseradish. Even infants drank it. Beer goes back to the Old Kingdom of Egypt and to Sumaria before that, and, possibly, as far back as 7000 B.C. Beer is made through boiling grain in water and was long recognized as safer to drink than water.

Safe drinking water was not commonly encountered in England. Streams and rivers were polluted by agriculture and especially by the towns and industries forming along their banks. Well water, even in small villages, was often compromised. On wine or beer, England operated on a 2% buzz.

Tea and coffee arrived in the early 1600s and, not much later, concentrated alcohol, gin. Italian monks had experimented with stills since around the year 1000, attempting to extract the "essence" from medicinal plants. Their experiments led to distilled alcohol.

Raspberries, currents, and blue berries might have been grown by the tribe in Lake Forest. It is not difficult to imagine Indians clearing away areas where berries grew or transplanting them to create "orchards." Hickories, which produce an edible nut, and sugar maples were often planted near dwellings, and in the warmer climate of 1000, Indians in Lake Forest might also have planted yaupon (Ilex Vomitoria). Yaupon is related to the plant from which mate, the Argentine drink, is brewed. Tea made from yaupon leaves is as rich in caffeine as coffee.

Along with planting pumpkin and squash, sunflower, and seedy plants like goosefoot and little barley, the Indians might also have transplanted roses. Twenty species are native to North America. As a tea or added to a stew, rose hips, rich in vitamin C, would ward off scurvy.

It would be interesting to determine if the Indians of Lake Forest had anything they could have converted into alcohol. It seems they did not, not until corn.

In Europe and in Central America (home to a non-stinging, honey-producing bee) honey was highly valued for its sweetness, its ability to heal wounds and preserve food, and, especially, for its convertibility into mead. However, in North America not one of over 4000 species of bees produced honey.

Lacy and Danzinger are of the opinion that mead, 10% alcohol, was the strongest drink available in England and drunk only by its wealthy. Yeomen might have equaled it with applejack, which is hard cider set out to freeze and then separated from its ice. But they may not yet have had apples. Some varieties of apples had been introduced by the Romans, but they did not do well in England's northern climate. Centuries later, French monks, by grafting one variety to another, produced apples with traits like cold tolerance, disease resistance, sweetness, and the size of both the fruit and the tree. Normans brought these apples into England following their successful invasion in 1066. A blended cider might include juice from a few "spitters," the small tart crab apples native to England.

Rabbits did not arrive until shortly after 1066. Turkeys came later from the Americas. But all the other domesticated animals found today on England's farms were there then in 1000. The Indians had the dog, just the dog, and they had brought that with them.

Because of their close association with so many domesticated animals, Europeans were rife with zoonotic disease. The Indians were not. They had lived with dogs for thousands of years, even before they crossed over into North America. By now they were well acclimated to what diseases a dog could transmit to a human. The diseases Indians could acquire from handling their killed game, such as giardia or tularemia, were few and were not transmissible from one person to another.

The first Americans brought head lice with them but not the body louse. The head louse does not transmit disease while the body louse can spread plague, typhus, and relapsing fever.

The body louse is actually a clothing louse. Genetic analysis indicates the separation of the body louse from the head louse occurred before the emergence of Homo sapien, indicating that Homo erectus, our immediate ancestor, wore clothing.

The first Americans also brought polio and herpes with them, but illness was rare among the Indians.

If Vikings spread disease to the New World during their visits in the 1000s, the Indian populations had recovered by the time of Columbus.

There may have been contact between the time of the Vikings and that of Columbus. Researchers found the curious log of an English vessel which left England bound for Ireland with a cargo of honey. The return was much later than would have been expected, and the return cargo consisted of long, straight lengths of timber. Honey was as common in Ireland as it was in England, and Ireland had long been deforested. Honey was unknown in North America and could have worked well to obtain cooperation from Indians while the English felled tall trees. Tall trees were highly valued in Europe for ships' masts, buildings, and watermills[4].

---

[4] Discovery Magazine article

There are other hints of contact from earlier times. The Kensington Stone is said to date from 1362, left by Scandinavians awaiting their doom after an Indian attack in what today is Minnesota. The Kensington Stone may be a fake, but it's difficult to believe that once the Vikings had established a route to the New World that others would not learn of it and follow.

By 1503, fishing fleets from France and other European nations were making annual contact with Indians in eastern Canada. Within twenty years the French were sailing up the Gulf of St. Lawrence as far as the Saguenay River to trade for furs. In 1535, Cartier sailed as far up the St. Lawrence River as an ocean-going vessel could reach, today's Quebec.

That winter the local Indians, Algonquins, saved Cartier and his crew from scurvy with tea they brewed from the inner bark of the white spruce. The French stayed eight years but then abandoned their attempt to establish a colony at Quebec. They did not return for sixty years. When they did, the Algonquins were gone, their land now occupied by the Hurons. The Algonquins' displacement may have been caused by disease they acquired from the French, but, more likely, the hunter-gatherers had been pushed aside by agriculturists, by corn-growers arriving from the south.

The ancestors of the English had domesticated a variety of animals. The viruses of these animals had done the same with them. Inherited immunity to these diseases was only partial. One quarter of England's children died of disease.

The Indians of North America lived largely without disease, and they had another advantage over the English in terms of health. They had better drinking water, especially in a location like Lake Forest, on the shore of the largest fresh water system in the world. Lake Michigan and Lake Huron are actually a single lake with a surface area of forty-five thousand square miles.

The Conquistador, Cortez, would have failed to conquer the Aztecs in 1519 if one of his slaves had not arrived in Mexico with an active case of smallpox. Much of the vast army of Aztecs opposing Cortez, and the rest of the Aztec population, died.

When the Pilgrims put ashore in 1620, Plymouth Rock was unoccupied. Nearby, they found many recently abandoned villages. Until a few years earlier, the shoreline of North America from Maine down through New York had been densely populated.

Then "The Great Dying" began, a period of illness which lasted two years and which may have killed 90% of the Indians living in the region. It was once thought this illness must have been plague, but now it is thought that the illness(es) may have been something so mild and ubiquitous among Europeans as to scarcely be noticed.

Thousands of years earlier, Indians had followed behind the glaciers as they retreated at the end of the last ice age. Some of the Indians entered into the area of Green Bay and Lake Winnebago. These early settlers had fish from Lake Michigan and smaller fish from the group of lakes and rivers which empty into the big lake. This vast marshland attracted great flocks of migrating birds twice each year, and twice each year, fish swam up from the big lake to spawn. Deer and bears were abundant. Finally, this area was one of the few and may have been the best in North America for the gathering of wild rice (Zizania palustris).

In terms of calories obtained for calories expended, wild rice may not have been the best grain in the world, but until the establishment of corn, it was the only grain in North America. Those who possessed it had something no one else had. It could be stored. It could be carried. It could support a larger population. With it, a tribe could withstand a siege or travel long distances to make war on an enemy. The closest thing to it might have been pumpkin and sunflower seeds.

This area of Green Bay and Lake Winnebago was, I imagine, larger than any of the small groups who first entered it could have controlled but that over time they formed a confederacy to keep out others who would covet this rich land. With stores of food on hand, more free time led to specialization of labor. The Indians of this region produced excellent pottery. They had no rivals, not until corn moved toward them, along the Ohio River around 800 A.D. and in Cahokia on the Mississippi River around the same time.

I imagine Lake Forest as occupied by Indians whose tribe had been pushed away or exiled by those living to their north around Green Bay and Lake Winnebago, permitted to live on the outskirts in exchange for allegiance. With access to lake fish, a band of forest, and wetlands to the west, Lake Forest would have been a desirable area, not as desirable as Green Bay and Lake Winnebago, but one still worth fighting to keep.

On the Mississippi River, the Indians at Cahokia kept improving their corn until it matured between frosts. Then,

Cahokia's population exploded. By 1000, Cahokia was as large as any city in Europe. With their corn, with 25,000 inhabitants, some say 50,000 at its peak, Cahokia would certainly have made its presence felt as far away as Lake Forest.

The yeomen in England plow their field even as they knew what destruction could come from a Viking raid or war with neighboring countrymen. Their fields might be burned, but if they did not plant, they were certain to starve.

The tribe in Lake Forest may have felt in a similar balance between faith and desperation. Their culture was very different from that of Cahokia. They spoke a different language. The tribe in Cahokia had come only recently from the south. They grew corn. They worshipped the sun and built enormous mounds. The Lake Forest tribe may have lived in the area for thousands of years. Living in small numbers, they had little of the sophistication that evolved at the vastly larger Cahokia, and very little of its power.

The confederacy of Green Bay and Lake Winnebago could have sent a force against the tribe in Lake Forest, but, having so much, they may never have asked for more than token tribute. Now, as the Lake Forest tribe attempted to continue living as they had for eons: planting, gathering, hunting, and fishing, they must have been ever more aware of Cahokia. By 1000, Cahokia could easily send out a war party of 100 or more. With stores of ground corn, they could stay in the field for weeks with no need to live off the land as they went. The tribe in Lake Forest was either falling into Cahokia's orbit or had already entered it.

In England, as inferred from surviving wills of the period, estate planning was common. Women were often named as heirs. They could hold property in their own name, manage it, and control the income derived from it. These rights were lost and not regained until the start of the twentieth century. Few women could read in 1000. Except for monks and priests, and maybe an abyss, very few could.

Latin, the language of the Church, was constant, but the language spoken outside the walls of the monasteries was changing. A Viking king had recently ruled England. The languages of the Vikings and the English were similar and beginning to merge. Then in 1066, the Normans invaded and this amalgam of Germanic languages was overladen with French, which the Normans, Vikings themselves only a hundred years earlier, had adopted.

Over forty languages were spoken in North America. Most of the tribes in the Northeast and Upper Midwest spoke a form of Algonquin. Francis Parkman, the nineteenth-century historian, wrote that the language of the Iroquois and Hurons differed from that of the Algonquins as much as English did from Hindi.

The language most likely spoken by the tribe in Lake Forest would have been that used by the ancestors of today's Lakota.

In the same way that English has changed since the time of Chaucer, a Lakota-speaker of today might find his ancestor's speech incomprehensible.

Indian women had rights and privileges under custom. Among the Iroquois, women choose half the sachems. Inheritance was matrilinear. It may have been like that in Lake Forest.

From early childhood, a girl in North America gathered greens and roots, tubers, fungi, the inner bark from some trees, and the leaves and buds from others. As she grew older, her tasks would include tending gardens, caring for younger children, cleaning and stretching hides, preparing game, baking, boiling, roasting, and preserving. The number of different animals and plants eaten was in the hundreds. One recorded recipe called for warmed animal fat to be whipped as it cooled until it grew frothy when berries, fermented greens, fish, and meat were to be added.

Using hides already prepared and softened, a young girl would learn to measure, cut, and stitch, make needles from bone and thread from sinew or plant fiber, use dyes, and decorate with porcupine quills, fringe, and colored thread. Two of the three types of dogs were likely under her care. She would be married after her first menstruation to a man twice or more her age. This marital practice was the same in England.

She would be included in a society or sisterhood. All tribes had societies of women. They held ceremonies separate from the men. Her husband married into her family. He moved into her family's dwelling. If they did not get along, he had to leave.

A headman of the village in Lake Forest may have held his position through prowess in battle, skill in hunting, or eloquence of speech. The eloquence of the Indians in expression impressed the French greatly. These headmen would have had counterparts among the women, ones who assigned tasks and settled disputes.

As my luck would have it, in 1991, an archeological dig had been conducted in Lake Forest and a village dating to the year 1000 was discovered.

Development of land west of Waukegan Road near the north branch of the Chicago River uncovered what had been a village in 1000 and evidence of previous use of the site going back 9000 years. The village was on top of a hillock in marshland to which fill had been added, and a palisade of pointed stakes dug in around.

Most of the tribe in 1000 may have lived in this fortified village, while other members stayed year-round at seasonal camps near the lake and along the crest of Green Bay Road. The distances were not great. From this settlement to Green Bay Road is perhaps three miles and, from there, another two miles down to the lake. Three miles to the west was the Des Plaines River. The river would have been navigable as far north as Lake Forest if fallen trees were removed. Further south, the Des Plaines River formed part of the traverse from Lake Michigan to the Illinois River. A party of warriors from Cahokia could ascend the Mississippi and then the Illinois River and be as close as Chicago in ten days' time.

Around this time, the year 1000, a small settlement may have started or started over again in what today is Northamptonshire, England. The village would take its name from the river which flowed past it. I had supposed that this village of Isham had formed because of a convenient ford on the narrow but swift-flowing Ise and because the river's velocity could be harnessed to power a watermill. Google Earth indicates the river may have been different in 1000. The Ise looks leveed most of its length. The river was wider and shallower in 1000 and would not have allowed heavy river traffic. It could not have been the setting for a large town. Fields were allotted to yeomen in long strips to minimize the turning about of the oxen. If the ford on the Ise was strategic, the yeomen of Isham likely included some of the local nobleman's best warriors.

Watermills had been in England for 1000 years. Over 5600 were recorded in the year 1086, roughly one for every 300 people. If a terrain provided a sufficient drop in elevation, water could be channeled away from a stream to push against blades attached to a pivot which, through gearing, spun one millstone on top of another. Designs grew more elaborate. Ponds were constructed to provide a uniform flow of water. The small distance between the stones could be adjusted to make the grind finer or courser. The power from the spinning shaft could be disengaged from the rotating millstone and used to sift the grain prior to grinding it. Waterpower was also used for other purposes, like lathes to make wooden cups and plates. More and more uses were found. By 1300, there were 17,000 water mills in England.

There were none in North America.

Wind-driven mills were introduced later by The Dutch in the 1600s. The Dutch built them to drain the Fens in southeast England for farming, and this led to the eradication of malaria which had existed in that low-lying area since the time of the Romans.

The tribe in Lake Forest may have ground the tiny seeds of pigweed and goosefoot together with the meal of pumpkin and sunflower seeds using simple grinding stones or a mortar and pestle. At Cahokia, the grinding of so much dried corn, in the absence of waterpower, would have needed a lot of labor. Prior to the arrival of the Europeans, use of waterpower does not appear to have ever existed in North America.

The Indians in Lake Forest practiced technology that was limited in its potential for innovation. Not much had changed in 1000 years except for the occasional readoption of the bow and arrow in times of strife. Little could be done to clubs or spears or hide preservation that had not been learned much earlier. Garden tools, cooking techniques, and clothing had all been worked out thousands of years before.

Speech may have been the best outlet for a creative mind.

March

In March, four yeomen are clearing land and sewing seed. Most of England's original forest had been converted into field and pasture.

It was different in North America. Indians created clearings by ringing trees and with fire, but without metal tools, they rarely cleared large sections. Even if they had the capability to remove the forest and create pasture, they had no animals to put on it. The eastern half of North America was an unbroken forest from the Gulf of Mexico north 1500 miles to where trees could no longer grow. From east to west, it was a thousand miles deep, extending in places hundreds of miles to the west of the Mississippi River. This region may have been more densely populated before the arrival of Old-World diseases, but before corn and beans, the population could never have matched those of Europe or Central America.

The absence of metal use in North America is one of the most striking differences between the Indians and the English. Nine thousand years earlier, on the shores of Lake Superior, 400 miles to the north of Lake Forest, Indians on the Keweenaw Peninsula were among the world's first to work with metal. Thousands of hammerstones were later found at the sites where mining companies began operations in the 1840s. The copper on the Keweenaw Peninsula and the surrounding area was 98% pure. A great deal seems to have been removed in earlier times, but by 1000, except as jewelry and as awls, copper was not part of Indian life. Some copper arrowheads and spearpoints from this era have been found, but not many. Copper awls were traded widely in North America as stone could not be shaped into an awl. A tribe may have specialized in producing them.

In not using copper points for their spears and arrows, did the Indians stop using a superior technology? Recently, an archaeologist, Michelle Bebber, constructed spear and arrow points of both stone and copper. She found the stone ones worked better.

Because of its purity, the Michigan copper contained no hardening alloys. Points and edges blunted easily. If used as an arrowhead or spearpoint, the greater weight slowed the copper ones in flight and diminished their penetration of a target[5].

There was no Bronze Age in North America. Even with a source of tin, some North American Cornwall, the Indians might never have added tin to their copper as they did not smelt. It was 98% pure to start with.

Large decorative cooper pieces have been recovered from Cahokia. If these pieces originated there, they could not have been made much after the year 1000. The great city was gone before 1400. By the 1600s, local Indians could not explain the vast ruins to the French.

---

[5] Michelle Bebber, American Archaeology Spring 2021

Also occurring in the year 1991 was an archaeological event of much greater significance than the discovery of the small Indian village in Lake Forest. A couple hiking high in the Alps came across a corpse It was determined that the body was that of a man who had died five thousand years earlier. Dubbed "Otzi," he is believed to have been one of those who came from the East with grain and livestock. He was fatally wounded by an archer and fell into a snowdrift or crevasse where his assailant could not reach his body. Among his possessions was a wedge of copper.

Otzi's assailant had used an arrow with a stone arrowhead, and Otzi had several in his quiver. Otzi's people were smelting copper from ore, having nothing comparable to the native copper of the Keweenaw Peninsula, but, perhaps for the same reasons as the Indians, they continued to use stone for the points of their spears and arrows.

The Indians abandoned the use of copper points, but they continued to produce copper "axe heads." These were not used as tools but as something which conferred or designated elevated status. Among Otzi's people, the copper wedge he carried may also have represented status. However, it was also an ice ax and a formidable tomahawk.

Eight years after Otzi's discovery the body of a young man was found at the foot of a retreating glacier in the St. Elias Mountains in British Columbia. He had died 600 years earlier. He wore a robe sown from pelts of arctic ground squirrels and a hat woven from conifer roots, which was described as quite beautiful. The young man had a spear, sweet cicely (for medicinal tea), and needles of mountain hemlock (also medicinal). In his stomach were chenopod seeds (pigweed or goosefoot). Judging by the plants he carried, he suffered from and died there of pneumonia. Corn did not grow this far north. The young man's people still depended on the same small seeds that the tribe in Lake Forest had needed to.

War was nearly constant in England. It was waged as much for slaves as it was for territory. People also passed into slavery through hunger or as punishment. Hierarchies existed: overseers, house slaves, field slaves, and the hapless souls sold to quarries or rowing galleys.

Slave-taking was common throughout the Mediterranean and along Europe's Atlantic Coast. Some Scots learned recently that their ancestors included Moors from North Africa. Moors had resettled in Spain following their invasion in 713. A few centuries later, some of their descendants were taken in a slaving raid on the Spanish coast. A Scottish noble bought them for his estate at the slave market in Dublin.

Dublin was a major slave market. It had started as a Viking settlement, a port where they bought captives brought from Ireland's interior. In earlier times, the clans of Ireland had stolen cattle from each other, but, by 1000, they were capturing members of rival clans to sell in the Dublin market.

Slaves paid for weapons. Weapons, more and better weapons, brought more slaves which would pay for still more weapons while seeking to protect one's own clan from capture. It was take-or-be-taken. It would happen again 500 years later in Africa.

Captives may have been kept as slaves in Lake Forest in the year 1000. In the 1600s, Pawnee slaves were kept by some tribes, but by then, most Indian men taken captive in the Northeast and as far west as Illinois were tortured to death. Women and children were slain.

In 1000, Indians in Lake Forest were in the midst of a great transition. The dominance of the tribes in the Lake Winnebago and Green Bay area was coming to an end, and that of Cahokia was rising.

At this time, only the pumpkin of the "Three Sisters" grew in northern Illinois and Wisconsin. The village was probably trying to grow corn but still needing to plant the old crops like pigweed, knotweed, goosefoot, and lambsquarter.

Cahokia had corn when others did not. As wild rice beat the small seeds, now corn beat wild rice.

The recent reintroduction of the bow and arrow in the region seems more indicative of warfare than of a change in hunting technique. Prior to corn, the land's human carrying capacity was determined primarily by how much animal protein and fat it could provide. Competition over these animals would create conflict, and the recent growth of Cahokia would have intensified it. Tribes southwest of Lake Forest, those between Lake Forest and Cahokia, would attempt to recoup the deer they needed to send as tribute to Cahokia, and some of the tribes might have been attempting to relocate. Either way, one tribe was pushed up against another, and conflict would emerge.

The site of the village near the north branch of the Chicago River, a slight stream this far north, was probably chosen for three reasons. For defense, the marsh provided the equivalent of a moat. The marsh was probably abundant in arrowhead (wapato) and cattail, which are both edible. Varieties of arrowhead grew all across eastern America in marshes like those along the Chicago River and the area just to the east where the Skokie Ditch runs today. Arrowhead leaves and rhizomes can be eaten from late spring and its tubers harvested in October. Cattails would have been abundant in the marshland, greatly enlarged by the work of beavers. Different parts of cattail are edible all year long. Third, the marsh was also where the great flocks of migratory birds put down every spring and fall.

The site in west Lake Forest is about three miles east of the Des Plaines River. If fallen trees were removed, the river would have been navigable from Chicago into Wisconsin. Warfare was constant in England in 1000, and yet trade flourished. It could have been the same in Lake Forest. Trade must have moved on the path which is now Green Bay Road or else the forest would have filled in and the path would have vanished. The path followed the highline between the ravines to the east which ran down to the lake and the marshlands to the west. Frequent settlement along this trade route from Chicago north past Green Bay seems likely, just like the string of towns which today lie along the Chicago Northwestern Railroad track.

For trade by canoe on the lake, or for fishing, or for warning of an approaching enemy, some settlement would have been kept at the lakeshore. The whole tribe might move to the beach to fish at different times of the year.

Geese, ducks, and cranes set down in the marshlands every spring and fall. Other birds nested there in summer. Passenger pigeons are estimated to have numbered in the billions. Cartier observed the passage of a flock in 1534. It took three days and darkened the sky. Wherever they put down, these birds provided an endless bounty.

In March, the Indians were reclaiming the borders of their growing areas from the ever-encroaching forest and prairie. It would have been a lengthy job without metal tools. To establish planting areas, even when starting with prairie sod rather than the forest, was a tremendous effort. Later, the European plow needed to be redesigned to break the sod of the Great Plains; it was so thick. Instead of oxen, teams of men were pulling plows of antler or fire-hardened wood through the heavy sod.

April

For yeomen, April included mass at Easter. Easter was one of the few times during the year when the priest shared the bread and wine with his congregants, bread and wine being too costly to distribute at communion every week. Fasting during the six weeks of Lent was necessity presented as a virtue, hunger sanctified, a blessing, an opportunity to express one's devotion to his Lord. When Lent ended, the full meal at Easter expressed optimism and regrowth for the coming year.

Hunger was less of a concern in Lake Forest. Spring brought forth a multitude of food sources. Migrating birds could be netted or snared, or brought down with a bolo or a stone from a sling. The passenger pigeon might descend in countless numbers. Fish traps offshore from the ravine runoffs on the lake or a weir across the Des Plaines River could have provided well. Greens would have been abundant. Eggs could be taken and mushrooms picked. Squirrels and rabbits were out of hibernation.

Other crops may have gone in earlier, but pumpkins and tobacco might have been planted later, in April, and berries, sugar maples, and hickories transplanted. Still, the Indians would have spent less time tending to their plants than the yeomen because fewer calories could come from them.

The Indians developed seeds of chenopods four times larger than those which grew wild. They developed sunflower seeds nearly a thousand times larger. The Indians tilled the soil, amended it, irrigated it, and prayed over it, but they did not have much to work with. Many animals made their way to their cooking fires, but all but one was wild and had to be hunted rather than taken from a pen or pasture. Dogs could haul cargo, but they could not pull a plow. The honeybee, a great pollinator, was not then in North America. Neither was the workhorse of the soil, the earthworm. It did not arrive until European settlers brought them in, probably with their first fruit trees.

Still, April for the Indians was not the time of anxiety it appears to have been in England when last year's supply of grain was starting to run low. A frost, an absence of rain, or an epidemic affecting the livestock could mean ruin for the yeomen. Sometimes they sold their children. It was legal. Mass suicides were recorded, many people joining hands and leaping together into the ocean. Cannibalism was not unknown.

The French recount Indians holding great feasts but at other times suffering severe scarcity. They found the Indians of New France interested in trade but at the same time at war with an implacable enemy, the Iroquois.

Control of the trade for beaver pelts would dominate life in the Northeast and Upper Midwest for the next two centuries. Life for Indians would never be the same. Beavers soon vanished from the lands of the Iroquois and

Hurons and the sources for their pelts moved steadily west and north until the beavers were nearly extinct.

Some of the Indians of New France came to worship the man on the cross. Almost side by side with the pious element of the French were the traders, men willing to go further and further into the wilderness in search of furs and perhaps Indian women and a freedom unknown to any peasant in France.

Liquor was introduced as a trade item early on. Within two hundred years, hardly any Indians would be living east of the Mississippi River.

Alcohol assisted, but, it was their greater numbers and their many diseases that carried the day for the Europeans. Disunity among the different tribes is often cited as a factor in their demise. Disunity was hard to overcome. Consider Europe when faced with the Viking raids. Rather than unite against the Vikings, most of the small kingdoms and principalities continued to wage war on each other. Pontiac, Little Turtle, Tecumseh, and Sitting Bull at different times did unite the tribes to oppose the Europeans. It made no difference.

Despite their long association, the French likely never understood the Indians, nor the Indians the French. The unstinting generosity of the Indians, their eloquence of expression, their steadfastness, bravery, stoicism, treachery, ritualistic torture, and cannibalism were all written about by the French. In the eyes of the French, the Indians were improvident. The Indians found the French to be stingy and unwilling to share. What else the Indians thought of the French can only be guessed. They may have seemed a good sort, if strange, what with those men among them who wore the dark robes: first, brown for the Recollect Brothers and then black for the Jesuits.

Initial contact with Indians living where today is Quebec was in 1535. The arrival of a large, sail-driven ship with white men onboard who wore unusual clothing and had firearms could not have surprised the local Algonquins. They must have been expecting it, having heard of the fishing fleets which arrived every year now at the mouth of the St. Lawrence River and others at Saguenay, halfway up the St. Lawrence, who traded for furs. The prospect of direct trade with the French may have been looked forward to with great anticipation.

In 1543, the French abandoned Quebec. They did not return for 60 years. Wars, rebellions, heresies needing to be suppressed, and disputes of succession which had to be resolved: these all took precedence over an endless forest. Without gold or silver, there was not much to recommend New France. It was not the abundant fish off the eastern shore. These had been harvested since the 1200s, and occupation of New France would not have added to the security of these fisheries so far to the east of Quebec. There were furs, though, and the fur trade brought adventurers and then settlers seeking land of their own.

Between 1543 and the return of the French to Quebec in 1603, Indians who grew corn had arrived from the south. Those who earlier had lived around Quebec and Montreal, the Algonquin hunter-gatherers, had been displaced by the Hurons. To the south were the Iroquois, and to the west were the Neutral Nation, the Tobacco Nation, and the Erie. These last five all spoke the same language. A legend shows accommodation at first between the newly arrived Iroquois-speakers, who were agriculturalists, and the Algonquins. The Iroquois speakers traded corn to the Algonquins for game and foods of the forest. Then they learned to hunt for themselves and drove off the Algonquins.

In time, the Iroquois destroyed the others.

Priests held great sway over the other Frenchmen, all screened before leaving France so that none would infect the New World with Protestant dogma. Some of the Frenchmen were like Joliet, who together with the Jesuit priest, Pere Marquette, "discovered" the Mississippi River. Joliet voyaged to the New World as a donee. Though not as priests, donees dedicated their lives to furthering the work of the Church. The priests were undeniably dedicated in their desire to win souls to Christ and break the grip that the devil so clearly held on these naïve savages.

The French did not trade firearms to the Indians, at first. If the French had a grand plan, which they did not, it would have been something like: keep the firearms to ourselves so that we retain an advantage and not encourage warfare among those whom we hope will provide us with furs forever while ceding their land to our arriving settlers. However, another European power, the Dutch, settled on the Hudson River not far to the south of the Iroquois, and they were quite willing to trade firearms for furs. In time, the Iroquois killed nearly all those whom the priests had labored to bring to Christ.

Settlers from Europe arrived yearly. They altered the landscape. It was not just with steel axes and saws. For thousands of years, the species of the North American forest had evolved to rely on the soil that surrounded them being covered with leaf litter. Earthworms in Europe benefitted farmers' fields by aerating them and converting mulch into castings. They had a different effect on North America's forests. Many species disappeared. The forests became unbalanced and thinned. Within fifty years of the arrival of the English at Jamestown, the game had left. The Indians of the region, the Powhatan, had needed to follow.

Unlike his English counterpart of 1000, at this time of year, the adult male Indian in Lake Forest was eating well, regaining weight he had lost over the winter. He would be busy maintaining or expanding planting areas while feeding on large migratory birds. Perhaps through trade along the Green Bay path, his people may have acquired seedlings for yaupon, and he was planting the seedlings, hoping they might get a good start before facing a hard winter. The seedy plants did not provide much nutrition, but their care requirements were minimal. More effort went into pumpkin mounds and tobacco and activities like tool production, curing hides, carrying in dirt in baskets, and erecting palisades.

By canoe on the Des Plaines River or along the lake, or down the Green Bay trail, there could have been active trade. One item may have been birch bark. It is light in weight and easily dragged by dog travois or carried by canoe. Its origin, in that warmer period, would have been far to the north. Using local material, canoes could have been constructed with elm bark, which is what the Iroquois used.

Salt, buffalo robes, tobacco, bearberry leaf, treated hides, dyes, medicinal herbs, seasonings, corn meal, shells of razor clams, obsidian, clays, copper awls, woven articles, dried fish, and possibly many other items might have been traded, if trade existed. The dog was the only available pack animal. Conceivably, a trading party with a pack of dogs, each pulling a travois, could cover fifteen miles a day and travel from Chicago to Marquette, Michigan in a little over a month, or all the way from Saline Springs in southern Illinois to the Keweenaw Peninsula and back in a summer. It would be possible if they and their dogs were fed along the way in the villages they passed through. In a world dominated by my imagined confederacy of tribes living in the Green Bay-Lake Winnebago region, such an open road of commerce would have existed. Compared to the postal system of the Inca, this would have been nothing.

May

In May, shepherds are tending their sheep. Indians had no sheep and, therefore, no wool. Indians raised some dogs for their hair, but they could not have provided much.

Dog-hair yard was used for decoration and perhaps for something small, like infant clothing.

An English yeoman's clothing was wool. Linen garments, made from flax, were expensive. Wool may seem itchy but is said to confer many benefits, including comfort. Without sheep and the wool they provided, Europeans would have had a difficult time inhabiting the northern part of their continent.

The material Indian women preferred for their clothing was deer hide. Their clothing was colorful, benefiting from a large choice of dyeing agents. For most of the year, a male Indian of the Eastern Woodland wore nothing except his moccasins. He might wear garments to protect against thorns and branches while hunting and in winter he would cloak himself in the hide of an animal, but, for most of the year, he was naked. Indian men did not lack for color, though, even without clothing. Tattoos, body paint, feathers, and ornaments in their hair and ears came in many colors.

English women used some of the same dyes as the women of Lake Forest. The English had coinage, banking, and taxes. Here, finding counterparts does not work as well.

Indians had waupun, objects which were highly valued and esteemed, but waupun was much more than coinage and was not used as such. A tribe at the mouth of the Chicago River might have kept warehouses for loads of salt coming from southern Illinois and for cornmeal, pottery, and buffalo hides sent up the Illinois River from Cahokia. If one tribe dominated another, tribute might be exacted. In the early 1600s, the Neutral Nation imposed a tax on the beaver pelts which the Tobacco Nation wished to carry across their land to trade with the French at Montreal.

In England, seventy mints operated under appointment by the king. Each was inside a stockade and offered safe deposit for the coins of local and visiting merchants. These mints issued two to four million fresh coins each year. The coins had end-dates and needed to be turned in for re-issue. The king's tax was collected by returning fewer coins than were received.

England was advantageously situated in climate and rainfall for the raising of sheep. Sheep were sheared in the spring, and the wool was washed, separated from plant matter, and spun into yarn. The practice went back to before the time of the Romans.

The yarn spun from the wool of England's vast flocks was gathered and moved to the port cities for further transport to mills in Belgium and Holland, or so it is assumed.

Most of what might have been learned about this trade was lost when Henry VIII's men closed the monasteries and burned the records going back centuries. The few that remain deal with trade in wine, furs, fish, and slaves.

The export of wool paid for the importing of furs and for the silver from Germany that was used in the coinage. The wine and fish were probably domestic. For much of England, slaves came from Wales, which was raided frequently.

The profit from the export of wool also had to cover the payments to the Vikings.

No part of England lies more than 60 miles from the sea. Vikings could ascend rivers in their long boats to raid almost anywhere. Their weaponry was state-of-the-art. So were their ships, navigation, and knowledge of coastlines. They were traders. They sought the young and fit and anything of value and killed and burned the rest. England paid heavily for peace, but the raids continued.

It was at this time that the English may have established a reputation for fair play. They agreed to allow the Vikings to cross a narrow causeway and draw up into a proper line of battle. Had they attacked the Vikings in the midst of their crossing, they could have destroyed them. But the English kept their word and were themselves destroyed.

England's king had hoped for support from the Normans just across the English Channel as he had married the duke of Normandy's sister, but no help came. He raised a navy, but it mutinied. He married off his daughters, still hoping for support, to no avail. Soon, a Viking ruled England.

If the yeomen prospered, their lord did too. He had responsibilities: administering justice, safeguarding the yeoman in their fields, collecting taxes, and preparing and arming his yeomen if needed to fight on behalf of the king. On coming into his inheritance, he needed to pay a tax to his king. Often, he needed to borrow to do so, and so started his lordship in debt.

A yeoman was a free man, but he could not leave his lord's domain without permission. He was a tenant farmer, allowed to keep a portion of his crop but also obligated to work on his lord's personal land. His lord's word was law. He could cut off your hand or hang you, although most punishment took the form of labor.

The "droit de seigneur" was a French tradition, say the authors, and not common in England.

A yeoman would be expected to attend mass where the priest would remind him that his king was chosen by God to rule over him and to act in his stead here on earth. The interests of church and state often intersected, but control by either was tenuous. Warfare was nearly constant and the Vikings annual visitors and often long-time occupiers of much of England.

The religious beliefs of Indians in 1000 in Lake Forest can only be guessed at. As understood by the French 600 years later, the world of the hunter-gatherer Algonquins was inhabited by multitudes of malicious spirits. Misfortune and illness were caused by demons which might be shouted away or propitiated with offerings. As hunters, the Indians gave thanks to the spirits of animals taken, and they may have prayed over their crops. A supreme deity might not have suggested itself until study of the sun developed through more advanced agriculture, when planting dates became very important. In the Americas, sun worship had evolved with the cultivation of corn and accompanied it on its thousand-year journey northward out of Mexico.

Yet, not long after year 0, way before the time of corn, Indians along the Ohio River were studying the heavens. Their astronomical knowledge was advanced and could not have been acquired except through decades of observation.

Until about 10,000 B.C., Indians could not have lived in Lake Forest. It was still under ice. The last advance of the glaciers reached its southernmost point around 18,000 B.C. The same advance occurred in Europe but held on longer in North America and, in particular, on what are today the Great Lakes. This period of intense cold had bound up the continent's moisture into a sheet of ice two thousand miles north to south, 3000 miles from ocean to ocean, and two miles high. South of the ice, the south half of the United States was a dust desert devoid of moisture. Canada and most of the United States was uninhabitable.

Plants and animals that had retreated south needed to regain a foothold before humans could enter the land. The Indians followed small birds like finches and sparrows north, gathering the same seeds they saw the birds eat. They would have eaten the small birds too. The Indians ate what was edible. Hunger educated them about mushrooms. Nuts, berries, and acorns after leaching, helped fill a diet. Knowing how to butcher and prepare hundreds of different animals and plants and the many uses for the hides, feathers, sinew, and bone had been acquired over countless generations.

A researcher figured that of 5,410 plant species existing at that time in the Eastern Woodland, Indians found uses for 2,100, and some of them had several uses.

A hunt was much more than the acquisition of meat. It bonded the men of the tribe, uniting them in purpose with something that was sacred and ancient. For the women, it was a constant and communal effort to extend the life of the tribe.

A Jesuit wrote of the male Indians as indolent, lying about smoking tobacco while the women hoed the gardens. Tobacco seems to have been a male thing. The priest described the Indian girls as wanton, taking lovers easily for gifts. Then, he wrote, the girls married, aged rapidly, and turned into hags. Tending cooking fires, weeding the gardens and collecting seeds all while bearing children at a young age must have taken a toll.

The summer equinox in ancient northern Europe I imagine as a bacchanalian event. Resultant pregnancies would produce babies born in the spring who would benefit from six months of growth before facing their first winter. Most of Europe lies north of Lake Forest. Seasonal variations in sunlight and the length of winter were more extreme. To give birth at the start of winter or in mid-winter in a Lake Forest warmer by several degrees than it is today might not have presented much additional danger to that already faced by Indian women and their infants at birth.

Whether Indian or English, a girl married around the age of thirteen and always to a man much older. The young woman might be accompanied by a dowry, or she might be purchased. Search for an alliance that would strengthen a family's position was often stronger than love. In England, a young girl might not meet the man who would become her husband until betrothment. Girls grew up with their fathers and then were married to men twice their age. Birth control was unknown or at least unreliable. Pregnancy, giving birth, midwifery to others, childcare, cooking, making clothing, and a hundred other tasks were hers.

Hierarchies existed. Women disciplined themselves, ostracizing one at a well or, in North America, quite literally, cutting off her nose.

Raising strong children was a primary objective. When she grew old, her husband would be dead, and she would need support from others. If she survived her pregnancies and other uncertainties of life in 1000, experience and wisdom might gain her influence.

The rights that an Indian woman held must have been regarded as very sacred. In 1650, an Iroquois warrior had been captured by the Erie. The woman, an Erie, had lost her brother in combat with the Iroquois. She had the right to keep the Iroquois to take the place of her brother. The captive would essentially be her slave, someone to hunt for her, help in her garden, someone who would support her as her brother would have. She also had the right to have the Iroquois tortured to death. This choice would earn her and her tribe the undying enmity of the Iroquois. Torture might last as long as three days. A captive, some were as young as ten, was expected to deport himself well, insulting his captors even as they sliced away strips of his skin to eat and force down his throat. At the end, if the Iroquois stood up well, his heart would be shared among the boys so that they, if such a day came, might show equal fortitude. They would drink his blood. Others of the tribe would share the rest.

The Eries pleaded with the woman that she accept the Iroquois as her brother. The Iroquois assured her he would serve her loyally and that should she exercise her right to kill him that his tribe would avenge his death. The woman chose torture. The Eries soon ceased to exist.

Women set snares and fish traps, and men had to know how to cook. Everyone had to know how to start a fire and build a shelter. A Huron woman written about by the French escaped her Iroquois captors in a canoe she built in an afternoon.

Simple pottery was practiced by many along the band of forest which ran from Chicago up past Green Bay. Going from simple clay pots to ones incised and painted, glazed, and even fired in a reducing atmosphere indicates leisure or at least some time off from searching for food. The best pottery in Illinois is found at Cahokia. Pots in which water could be boiled existed at this time in Utah, and this development helped lead to the inclusion of beans in the diet of the Indians. Beans and the pottery to boil them in arrived in northern Illinois about two hundred years later. Prior to 1200, hides formed like a pocket and held up by stakes had been used as kettles. Fire-heated rocks dropped into the water produced a rapid boil. This practice probably went back to before the crossing of Beringia. A pit must have been dug deep enough for the top of the suspended kettle/hide to be level with the ground surrounding it. Then a fire could be lit next to the hole to heat the stones so that when they were hot, they could be pushed over the rim and into the water. Alternatively, using two long green boughs the heated rocks could be lifted over the rim of the hide.

Diet among the Indians varied by region and over time. Where both were available, buffalo was favored over venison. The preference may reflect more than taste. Buffalo robes provided unequaled warmth, and buffalo were easier to hunt than deer or elk. Before the Indians acquired horses, they cloaked themselves in wolfskins to crawl close to the dim-sighted buffalo and then shoot an arrow into the soft spot behind the shoulder. They also chased the buffalo into marshes, dead-end canyons, and off cliffs. A deer provided less meat and spooked quicker in a hunt, but deer hide made the best clothing and moccasins. Some tribes consumed a lot of seed, but on the Great Plains, almost all the calories came from game. One tribe preferred to feed buffalo to their dogs and then eat the dogs.

By 1653, the Iroquois had killed nearly all the Hurons, including those of the Neutral and Tobacco Nations. One band of Hurons had escaped and fled far to the west to the furthest of the Great Lakes, Lake Superior. The Iroquois went after them. They left their villages in upper New York state, descended to Lake Ontario, crossed the lake, and by many portages reached Lake Huron, crossed it, and portaged up to Lake Superior to set off along its southern shore. This is a distance of more than 700 miles. Had they needed to rely just on what they could hunt or fish for along the way, they could not have made the journey. They had pemmican at the start, but most of the trip would have been fueled by corn.

Corn made it possible. It was not just supplying the men in the war party. The tribe would also have to go without the men's labor for the summer. Equipping this war party must have been extensive. They needed canoes of the best quality and paddles, shelters, blankets, weapons, and baskets of parched corn. The Iroquois had sent word in advance. They were coming that summer to kill every

Huron and every member of the small band of Chippewas who had given the Hurons sanctuary on their land.

Seven hundred years earlier in England, Vikings had caused similar fear, descending suddenly to destroy ports and villages on England's coast, pillaging, raping, burning, and slaughtering. The Saxons had not paid what the Vikings had demanded.

Vikings dominated western and northern Europe in 1000. In 1066, Harold, England's last Saxon king, had needed to fight off a Viking attack on England's northeast coast immediately before hustling his army south to face the invading Normans. A century earlier, as invading Vikings themselves, the Normans had made themselves masters of northwestern France. The reach of the Vikings is astonishing: from Canada to the Volga, from Greenland to the Mediterranean.

Half a world away, the Polynesians were discovering every inhabitable island in the Pacific Ocean (Hawaii 940, Tahiti 1000, and New Zealand in 1320).

Among the many activities of the Indians who lived on the Great Lakes, sailing is absent. Indians sailed on Puget Sound but not on the Great Lakes. The Polynesians sailed great distances on boats made without metal tools. Perhaps, the bark canoe was just difficult to improve upon, especially where so many portages were needed. These slender, lightweight vessels with crews of seven or more could cover great distances in a single day. In the same way Julius Caesar had his men row when sail was an equal option, to keep them strong; imagine what paddling from a kneeling position for ten hours a day did for the upper body. The Iroquois who pursued the small bands of Hurons and

Chippewas on Michigan's Upper Peninsula would wield their war clubs with authority.

Still, the absence of sail argues that there was not much trade on the Great Lakes. Food and material for clothing and shelter were all close at hand. Indian sites have been found with items which could only have originated from sources a thousand or more miles away, but until the Europeans came seeking furs, there may have been no bulk trading, except for salt and tobacco.

As far back as anything else found in the eastern United States is evidence of tobacco use. "Nicotiana quadavalis," which was either native to the Upper Midwest or else brought across from the Pacific Northwest, was the first in use, but well before 1000, nicotiana quadavalis was displaced by "nicotiana rustica." Nicotiana rustica is the only plant species Indians ever took across the Isthmus of Panama into North America. Its nicotine content is three to nine times that of current-day cigarette tobacco. Every tribe in North America smoked it. For some, it was the only crop they planted. Forty or more varieties were developed. Some could induce hallucinations. Smoking tobacco was an ancient, almost organic practice. The ceremony included the tobacco mix, the pipe, the grinder, and the pouches for them. A man's tobacco pouch was often all that he wore. Tobacco was central, essential as an offering of peace and hospitality. It was part of any celebration or to invoke spirits or ask for their wisdom.

"The Savages produce a prodigious amount of tobacco," wrote a Frenchman in 1719 upon visiting the Wichitas, a tribe living on the Great Plains west of the Mississippi River. They may have traded tobacco along the

Mississippi. De Soto in 1540, wrote of Indians who plied the Mississippi River in large canoes, trading salt from the giant domes in what today is northern Louisiana.

Neither wine nor silver were traded by Indians in Lake Forest in 1000. The closest significant amounts of silver were in Colorado, 900 miles to the west, and not used by anyone much north of Mexico.

For nearly the whole time they were in North America, the Indians may have had no way of creating alcohol. Corn could have changed that. Corn changed Indian society. The mounds at Cahokia represent a lot of calories. The inhabitants of Cahokia obtained these calories from corn. They were also consuming a lot of deer in the year 1000, disproportionately the choicer parts. Whole deer and the best parts of others were being sent to the city from outlying tribes.

Cahokia's site had been sculpted by floods and then covered in deposits of rich silt. It would also have benefited from being next to the weather-modulating Mississippi River, three-quarters of a mile wide at that point. The site must have impressed the early corn-growers from the south, if only they could coax the corn to mature between frosts. Once the corn adapted, Cahokia's growth was rapid. Corn was power.

June

June shows a lot of activity. A pair of oxen stands by as one man fells a tree and another loads a length of timber onto a cart. By 1000, most of England's forests had been converted into pasture and cropland. What forest remained was managed carefully. A mature forest represented a considerable inheritance. Large trees were in demand for dwellings, bridges, ships, and watermills. Smaller pieces were made into implements, and the scrap was burned for heating. The best went for charcoal which, with billows, made blacksmithing possible. Every species had uses. Oak was best for pillars and yew for bows. (Otzi's bow was made of yew). Wood from Italian yew trees was the best. Rights to firewood, the gathering of mushrooms and eggs, and the taking of small game were often specific. An English forest was well picked over.

The oak forest, which stretched from Chicago north past Green Bay, was 200 miles long and extended inland, interspersed with wetland and meadows, to the Mississippi River and beyond, and this stretch of forest was just part of the northwest portion of the vast Eastern Woodland, two million square miles of forest. England, Wales, and Scotland together are 89,000 square miles, and the acreage of its forests at this time was a great deal less than that. In England, timber was fast disappearing and quite valuable. In North America, the Indians of the Eastern Woodland were almost lost in it.

In England, towns were forming around the stockaded mints. Markets became established inside and then along the outer walls of the stockades. Trades became more defined, and better products were produced. Towns absorbed the surplus population from outside, but in times of disease, urban populations fell quickly. Obtaining good water was hit or miss, and removing night soil and garbage was difficult in tight quarters.

Trade was sophisticated, though. In 1000, the town of Droitwich was England's largest producer of salt. The saltworks were owned by stockholders who lived all around England and even included a church in Paris. Real estate developers operated. Tourism of a form existed, centered on the veneration of the bones of saints.

International trade predated 1000. When he died in 735, the Venerable Bede had among his possessions peppercorns from the East Indies. By 1000, silks, ivory, and fine gold jewelry from Italy could be purchased in England. The transport of goods around England was mostly by boat. Shallow-draft boats could reach most towns. The roads were in poor shape, much worse than how the Romans had left them. Larger craft were used on the open sea. Those of the Vikings were eighty feet by fifteen. Five hundred years later, Columbus's flagship, the Santa Maria, was nearly the same length and width.

Trade existed in the New World, but geography put it at a great disadvantage. The apple, for instance, traveled from its origin in the Caucasus Mountains westward, all the way to England and Ireland. It traveled along the same zone in climate. The horse, domesticated far to the east, was also brought westward without difficulty. However, in the New World, the Isthmus of Panama was the only land passage between North and South America. It was narrow, out-the-way, and mosquito-infested.

A second disadvantage for all Amerindians was the improbable difference, New World vs Old, in the number of animals which could be domesticated. In the New World, only four or five ever were. The Muscovy duck was raised by Indians from Brazil to Mexico. This bird and the dog were the only domesticated animals brought across the isthmus in either direction.

In the Andes Mountains of South America, the guanaco was developed by Indians into the alpaca, the vicuna, and the llama, or, alternatively, the llama was developed from the guanaco and the alpaca from the vicuna. Either way, the domesticated animals were never brought across Panama to similar locations in the mountains of North America. Differences of climate and elevation from the Andes through Panama were too great. Indians in northern South America raised guinea pigs, but not even these small animals made it across the isthmus.

The turkey was the only animal ever domesticated in North America, first in Central America and centuries later in the American Southwest.

Corn crossed the isthmus north to south. Its origin was not far to the north of Panama. However, not cassava, tomatoes, or potatoes ever crossed the isthmus to North America, making the passage of nicotiana rustica all the more impressive. Sweet potatoes in various forms are now thought to have been native from the southeastern United States down through the Caribbean, South America, and out over the Pacific, and that early on, Indians, Polynesians, and later, Europeans hybridized them. Wild sweet potatoes native to the American Southeast were collected by the Indians, but the domesticated variety from the Andes never came north until introduced by Europeans.

The Columbian Exchange is an interesting concept, the sudden exchange of plants and animals from the New World to the Old and from the Old to the New. Corn to the Pilgrims, barley to the Wampanoags, potatoes to Europe, wheat to the Americas.

As well as East/West, though, the Exchange was also North/South.

Nicotiana rustica continues to be grown throughout the world, although the most popular tobacco is "nicotiana tabacum." The early Spanish and English explorers/ invaders killed nearly all the Indians who lived on the islands of the Eastern Caribbean and replaced them with slaves they purchased in Africa. Their plantations grew sugar but also cotton and nicotiana tabacum, which the now-extinct Indians had developed. By the late 1700s, this plant, developed by the exterminated Indians and now grown on plantations in the North American colonies by slaves brought from Africa, was sold to the Indians of North America at a price made so low through the use of the slave labor that the Indians traded for it rather than continuing to grow their own.

In North America, tobacco had been used for thousands of years before nicotiana rustica arrived. "Nicotiana quadravalis" and possibly "nicotiana northwesticus," if not grown as far east as Illinois, reached there by trade. Nicotiana rustica contains much more nicotine and displaced the varieties native to North America. To the tobacco Indians added other plant material, but not cannabis of any stripe. It is all Old World. Bearberry would not have grown in Lake Forest but might have been available through trade with tribes living to the north. CPC-type behavior has been associated with smoking its leaves, but bearberry is frequently mentioned as being added to the tobacco. Also mentioned is sumac, possibly as a sweetener. The Lakotah in the 1840s always added the bark of red willow. Datura, known as Jimson weed or locoweed, was occasionally added. Accepting a calumet, a pipe of peace, came with certain considerations.

On their descent of the Mississippi River in 1673, a calumet saved the lives of Marquette and Joliet and their party on two occasions. The calumet had been given to Marquette by a chief of the Illinois and it acted as a passport. Pere Marquette held the calumet aloft, and each time the tribesmen who had been threatening stopped and, instead, led Marquette and his party to their villages where they feasted them for days. At this time, relations between tribes on the Mississippi River must have been peaceful and food plentiful. The chief of the Illinois was able to grant Marquette safe passage on the Mississippi. His calumet was recognized and respected by tribes of different languages living hundreds of miles downstream.

Trade was natural to the Indians. It was both the benefactor and the promoter of peace. Trade redistributed resources from where they were plentiful to where they were scarce, allowing a greater population and a higher standard of living. As an Iroquois chief observed, "Trade and peace, we take them to be one thing."

July

July in England was when fodder was cut and set aside. Much of England's plowed acreage went for fodder. Winters were milder and snow cover might not have been a problem in pasturing the sheep over winter. The fodder would have been mostly for the oxen. The crop in this scene does not look like hay. More likely, the artist drew legumes commonly known as "vetches." Today's livestock are fed corn and soybeans, but these were not available in 1000. Vetches may be making a comeback, though, as a more sustainable source of animal food.

Not shown in the Julius Work Calendar but almost certainly present in villages were donkeys and goats. Donkeys cannot pull a plow but can carry a substantial load or a person at a faster than walking pace. Goats were often put with a herd of sheep as goats would eat plants sheep would not and, in that way, help conserve a pasture.

In the hundred years that followed 1776, white settlers packed their goods in wagons pulled by draft animals and moved west at a pace of about twenty miles a year. They settled every part of the lower forty-eight states, pushing aside earlier inhabitants. Most of the wagons pulled across the Great Plains in the 1840s were pulled by oxen.

Oxen would not run off, Indians had little interest in stealing them, and, unlike a horse, when they could work no longer, they were still valued for their meat. Francis Parkman's account of his visit to the Great Plains in 1846 recounts emigrants losing horses to the Indians. A large herd of beef cattle also went missing that summer. Some of the emigrants carted items like mahogany bureaus as far west as Wyoming before abandoning them upon seeing the mountains that lay ahead.

The fort at Laramie was run by the American Fur Company, not the U.S. government. The nearest cavalry was 700 miles east in Leavenworth, Kansas. It was the "Wild West." Fur traders, Indians, their dozens of children, Canadians, Mexicans, emigrants passing through, many of them Mormons, with no real law, just a lot of commerce at the fort. That year the Dakotah and Crow waged war on each other, the ill-fated Donner Party passed through Fort Laramie, and the war with Mexico started.

For the yeomen in England, the needs of their livestock over the coming winter needed to be focused on in this last month before the harvest, even as each of them was calculating what rations yet remained for him and his family. Grain which in good years was fed to the hogs, in bad years was sold at ever-increasing prices. Adjunct to poverty was drug use. The worst of the rye, the smelly, moldy stuff, all that was left, might be used. The mold could include rye ergot, the source of LSD. As recently as the 1950s, a baker's batch of rye bread put a Swiss town into a craze for almost a week. Wheat-eaters weren't safe, either. Darnel somehow escaped the notice of the drug experimentalists of the 1960s. Darnel is wheat's evil twin.

It is the tares in Jesus's parable about the landowner whose steward asked, "Did we not plant good seed?" Darnel is similar in appearance to wheat and cannot readily be separated until both are nearly ripe. Then one can be harvested and taken to the threshing floor while the other is put to the flames. Should darnel be harvested along with the wheat and baked into bread, the consumers are in for some unexpected perspectives, and this did occasionally happen until about the 1850s. But not all darnel cleared from the fields in July was burned.

Some of the yeomen ate bread made with darnel, moldy rye, cannabis, and poppies. It was called "crazy bread."

No great epidemics are recorded for the period, but in England, one in four children never make it to adulthood. There were wars and raids, occasional famine, and the many diseases brought on by their close contact with domesticated animals as well as the mice, rats, fleas, and lice that lived with them. Sanitation practices which worked well enough in small villages often failed in towns, and the industrial waste grew year by year.

The rivers and streams of England were dying, its fish vanishing. Fishermen had to adapt. They went out into the bays and estuaries, and then further and further in larger and larger boats. By 1000, some were fishing as far away as the Orkney Islands north of Scotland. By the 1200s, European fishermen were taking fish at the Grand Banks, not far to the east of New England and eastern Canada.

England's social system at that time has been described as consisting of those who worked, those who fought, and those who prayed.

Thirty monasteries were scattered across England. Some had vast land holdings and acted as agricultural colleges. Others had associated cathedrals, libraries, and hospitals. The chanting of monks, day and night, was part of life in any town with a monastery. Their lives were ruled by clock-candles. Matins at 2 in the morning were followed by prime at 6. Five more periods of prayer followed, ending at 7 PM, bedtime. Study and contemplation were how life was best spent. Monks were read to while they ate. Sometimes, they were whipped. The monasteries and nunneries absorbed much of the orphaned and destitute. Some nunneries and monasteries operated side by side, with a wall down the middle and always presided over by a female blood relative of the king.

Mid-summer in Lake Forest may also have been a time of shortage. No migrations were in progress. The fish were probably at the bottom of the lake but might reappear if a thunderstorm flooded the ravines. Squirrels, rabbits, and hares might be snared. (The European rabbit, originally from China, could be domesticated but was not then in England. The American rabbit, the cottontail, could not be domesticated.) Deer or a bear might be taken but more likely were mid-sized game: raccoons, beavers, porcupines, and even skunks, augmented by berry-picking and mushrooming, capturing frogs and turtles, and gathering cattails. Otherwise, it was a diet of seeds. Or perhaps netting swallows by the bluff: edible and always there, but maybe a last choice.

Clothing for children was as minimal as it was for men. Mosquitos would have been abundant.

Mosquito-eating birds would have been too. Still, the mosquitos would get through. How did naked men and children defend themselves and the women too when they were away from the smoke of the cooking fires? They may have slathered their skin with something like bear grease. Sunflower seed oil is also mentioned. Another possibility is that the human body can defend itself. Producing sweat that could repel mosquitoes might be within the capabilities of the human body, especially if aided by the consumption of herbs discovered during the prior 15,000 years and more of dealing with insects of the New World.

When the last ice age ended and the oceans of the world rose, Tasmania became separated from the rest of Australia. The gap grew wider year by year. Some of the Aborigines moved uphill, and the rest onto what became Tasmania. The hilltops became the Flinders Islands and were occupied for about 1500 years, close to a hundred generations in isolation before the Aborigines there died out. The Aborigines who remained in Tasmania dropped the use of clothing, and then of fire.

Temperatures in Tasmania in mid-winter go well below freezing. Early European visitors saw Aborigines diving after ducks in frigid water and then eating them raw.

Dealing with mosquitoes might not have been too great a challenge. The mosquito-borne diseases of malaria and yellow fever had not yet reached the Americas. The English would introduce malaria at Jamestown. Yellow fever came later with the slaves from Africa.

South of Lake Forest, in the warmth of the year 1000, the presence of yaws might not have been very far distant. Yaws is the mosquito-borne disease generally thought to be the progenitor of syphilis, whose origin, New World or Old, is still in debate. Syphilis is caused by a spirochete, a spiral-shaped bacterium. It was the "Great Deceiver" in nineteenth-century medical literature, the damage of the spirochetes presenting in one part of the body before their effects showed in others.

Like its cousin, Lyme Disease, syphilis is a single disease that can cause many afflictions. Initial symptoms are often overlooked, and the realization of infection might not occur until years after exposure. Indians in the Bahama Islands suffered from yaws, which causes a skin rash and then damage similar to that caused by syphilis. It spreads through contact as well as by mosquitoes. After arriving in the Bahamas, some of Columbus's crew may have become infected with the disease and brought it back to Europe. Yaws may have already progressed into syphilis before Columbus arrived, or maybe yaws combined with a European spirochete. In any case, syphilis was very much in evidence and first described in Naples in 1494. By 1900, 6% of Germany's population suffered from it. It was probably the same throughout Europe. If syphilis originated in the Bahamas, it is the only disease known to have infected the Old World from the New.

August

In August, seven yeomen are hard at work. The harvest season was short, and every hour of daylight needed to be used. When all the grain was in, Lammas, the feast with bread baked from the newly harvested grain, was held. Yeomen, as they ate the soft, fresh bread, knew the results of the harvest and what it meant for the coming year. The loaves were sloping round paddies and coarse. They would turn rock-hard and keep for weeks, added to soups or stews where they would soften. Wheat bread was the most popular. Wheat, rye, and barley are closely related and all had seed-heads many times larger than anything available to the Indians of Lake Forest.

Lacey and Danzinger think August must have been a particularly smelly time of the year in England with the odor of excrement everywhere. The frequent rains of spring would have ended, and the streets of villages and towns would have become coated with the droppings of cattle, horses, and herds of sheep.

Archaeologists who have examined latrine deposits of that period deduced that diets were high in vegetables and protein and that diarrhea was prevalent. Moss was the preferred material for afterward. Bathing, whether by rich or poor, was infrequent.

Intestinal parasites were common in England, and parasites did not limit themselves to the intestines. The maw worm, which Otzi also suffered from, can exit from the eye. Europeans of the Middle Ages are often portrayed as filthy and parasite-ridden, but some historians dispute that.

In one of his novels about the northwest frontier of America in the 1750s, the author, Kenneth Roberts, described how two men rid themselves of lice. They walked along a riverbank until they came to an anthill. They took off their clothes and lay them by the anthill and then bathed in the river. Ants swarmed over the clothing and carried away the lice and their eggs. When the men emerged from the river, they waited for the ants to finish, put their clothes back on, and now, refreshed and cleansed of lice, continued on their way. It is interesting to think that English villages of the tenth century may have had de-lousing stations.

The heavy use by Indian women of sunflower oil on their hair may have been to counter head lice. Indians did not harbor body or pubic lice until they met the Europeans.

The population density of the Northeast and Upper Midwest could have been much greater than what the French observed in the 1600s, but it could never have matched that of England where wheat, barley, rye, and oats further north, in combination with draft animals and metal plows could produce so many more calories per acre and per hour of labor. With neither European grain nor corn nor beans available, the population of Lake Forest in 1000 had a much more restricted upper limit. Along the southern shore of Lake Superior, three hundred miles to the north, one scientist estimated that 200 square miles was needed to support a single human[6]. If this estimate is accurate, only 82 Indians could have survived in what today is Michigan's Upper Peninsula. The extensive mining operations in ancient times would have required importing food. With corn still a long way off, it is interesting to consider how the miners feed themselves.

What was the human carrying capacity in 1000 of what now constitutes the city of Lake Forest and its neighbor, the village of Lake Bluff, 21 square miles in total? East of Green Bay Road, the forest runs downhill to the lake. To the west lay more forest but with prairie and marshland interspersed. The present-day Skokie Ditch did not then drain the area and beavers would have built it up to hold as much water as possible, creating a region which would have supported a multitude of turtles, frogs, crayfish, cattail, and arrowhead, all edible.

Whitefish and lake trout swam up the Fox River every fall to spawn. Smaller runs also occurred on the Milwaukee and Chicago rivers. In the spring, walleye and sturgeon swam up the same streams. A dozen other species lived in these waters year-round, including good-sized fish like bass and muskie. Unless by custom or invited, the Lake Forest tribe would not have been at these semi-annual banquets, having to rely on what lay off their own shoreline. If a fish species migrated seasonally around Lake Michigan, the Indians were taking advantage of it.

However, venturing any distance out onto Lake Michigan was a serious undertaking. Storms can come up

---

[6] Fred Rydholm, "Michigan Copper"

out of nowhere, causing canoes to capsize or break apart under the continuous pounding of waves. In the 1650s, a war party of Iroquois drowned while attempting to cross the lake. In more recent times, many large vessels have capsized, been dashed onto rocks, or ripped open in seas reaching as much as a reported forty feet from crest to trough. Saltwater sailors have been shocked by the violence of storms on the Great Lakes. Freshwater waves come on much more quickly than do those on the ocean. Since the 1600s, over 10,000 vessels are known to have been lost on the Great Lakes[7].

To be a tribesman in Lake Forest, one had to be able to build and handle a canoe, track animals, lance a bear, pull a furrow, build shelters and start fires, net birds, or hit them with stones from a sling. If one could also make bows and arrows and develop the skill needed to make this hunting device/weapon worth using, he would be a valued member of his tribe. Archery had been practiced in England for thousands of years before the arrival of the Romans. In North America, between 15,000 B.C. and 1000 A.D., the bow and arrow was adopted and abandoned many times and, around Lake Forest, recently taken up again.

A shaft sharpened and fire-hardened at one end and shoved, thrown, or thrown further with an atlatl goes back to well before 15,000 B.C. Neanderthals used spears. So did the Romans who also did not make much use of the bow and arrow. The Romans had two types of spears, one to be thrown as the battle was being joined and a longer one to thrust with, the man using the spear protected by others of

---

[7] William Ratigan, 'Great Lakes Ship Wrecks and Survivors'

his legend forming a shield wall in front of him. When an opening formed, he would thrust, most often at legs and feet.

Behind the front line, interspersed with reserves, were corps of slingers. The most skilled came from the Balearic Isles off Spain's southern coast. The Romans, the real pros of war, used two different "stones": ceramic ones for use at a distance and metal ones for close quarters. Equipping a slinger was cheap, but, if protected, a slinger could take out a fully armored front-line opponent. A stone hurled from thirty yards could crush an unprotected forehead and might still kill if hitting a helmet.

The spear and the sling were easily made. Constructing a bow and arrow was more complicated.

A straight shaft with an arrowhead at its tip, guided by glued-on feathers, and propelled by bent wood and stretched tendon – it was a lot of parts. The bow and arrow might be advantageous in certain hunting situations, but was it worth so much effort?

In villages of 1000 in Lake Forest and in England, practice with the sling, spear, and bow and arrow may have been constant as so much depended on acquiring the necessary skill and strength.

In 1346, at the Battle of Crecy in France, the bow and arrow was decisive. The English bowmen, not much more expensive to kit out than a corps of slingers, destroyed the armored, mounted French knights, the focus of years of France's military spending. Forts were also built, of course, but a lot had been invested in the knights. Their armor, 70 pounds for an average-sized knight, was extremely costly, as were their steeds, which were also armored. Each knight had to be taught to ride and then to ride with armor and a lance. More training was needed to learn to fight as units, and every knight and horse required attendants, leatherworkers, and blacksmiths.

At two hundred yards out, the English archers began to shoot, and their arrows pierced the best armor France could produce. The French knights were annihilated. For centuries the bow which could propel an arrow through armor at 200 yards was a mystery. Then archaeologists recovered some from a barge found sunken in the Thames River. The pull-weight of a bow used by a modern bow hunter is around 50 pounds. The pull-weights on the bows recovered from the barge were between 190 and 215 pounds. Hitting a deer with such force might spoil the meat, but that was the sort of bow that was needed to pierce the French armor. The great proficiency of the English archers may have resulted from an edict which forbad all sports in England, except archery. The bowmen at Crecy had been recruited from all over England. Picture the guys in the weight room who warm up at the bench with two or even three plates at each end of the bar. It was a pairing of 4000 strong men with bows and arrows to match.

Seventy years later, at the Battle of Agincourt, English archers again destroyed the French knights. This time the French fought on foot, and their armor was stronger and included scalloping to deflect arrows. It was expensive. The armor could be held for ransom as well as the man who had been wearing it.

The English archers worked in groups of five. Each group carried long staves, machetes, and mallets. In front of their positions, to hold off cavalry, they would sharpen the staves and drive them into the ground at about a 30-degree angle and then sharpen the ends sticking out into points.

Unwisely, the much larger French army accepted battle on a narrow front, one which favored the English, a ridge hemmed in by forest and approached only through a soggy meadow. The front was so narrow that most of the French knights were backed up, unable to be at the front. The knights who were at the front had to slog through mud knee-deep to get at the English and then were so pressed from the rear that some fell forward, were stepped on, and in their heavy armor, drowned in the mud.

The English archers set up on the flanks of the few armored English knights. The struggle at the front was static, the French knights not able to make headway against the English knights. Before long, the archers exhausted their arrows, but not before they had tired the French knights who had been holding their shields over their heads the whole time to fend off the arrows. Now, using their bows and staves, the archers, brutishly strong men, advanced on the French flanks, catching at their feet. At first, the French knights held formation and refused to engage with the English rabble, but then as dozens of their comrades were being dragged away by the archers, the French panicked and fled the field. English archers grew wealthy that day.

The English longbow was a fearsome weapon, but the Indians of Lake Forest may have had no use for something so powerful or for any bow at all. For long periods, Indians in North America forewent the use of the bow and arrow. For hunting ducks or geese, an arrow was too valuable to risk losing in a marsh. Nets, slings, or bolos would have been used. For game in the forest, snares or a lance sufficed.

As with good pottery, some leisure was needed for the development of archery. The bow and arrow might have been used to its best advantage in warfare. A shot from a bow is made more quickly than loading a stone into a sling, and slings work best in the open, not in a forest. The recent re-adoption of the bow by Indians in this region probably indicates warfare.

Although made without metal tools, the bow and arrow of the Indians was still formidable. As late as 1840, out to fifty yards, the Indian bow and arrow was described as "accurate as a rifle." In exchange for furs, the Indians traded for axe heads and kettles, for decorative beads, for sugar, for liquor, and for other things, but not for the French bow and arrow.

Before he died from the arrow which pierced his back and severed an artery, Otzi had been engaged in a furious battle. Within a forty-hour stretch, he had descended 10,000 feet and then climbed back up. He appears to have slain three opponents with his bow. If so, Otzi's battle was one of three successful ambushes, followed by the one which was not. Following each of his kills, Otzi had pulled his arrow free from his opponent's body, leaving the arrowhead behind. Otzi's killer may have done the same as the arrowhead embedded in Otzi's skeleton was not attached to a shaft. If it was an enemy who pulled the arrow free, why didn't he also take with him Otzi's valuable copper ax head? It may have been a fellow tribesman who pulled the arrow from Otzi's back and then, when Otzi bled out, threw his body into a crevasse where the enemy could not get at it.

September

In September, two young men are driving hogs through a forest. A hunt is in progress. The men carry spears. They are nobles, judging by their dress and especially by their dog, which looks like a greyhound. Hunting dogs were expensive to train and keep.

One of the men is holding a horn to his lips. They are part of a larger group of hunters to whom they are signaling and driving the hogs toward. The chapter is entitled "Pagans and Pannage."

"Pannage?"

Animals were culled in September. In most years, meat was plentiful, especially mutton.

Chickens were already in England when the Romans arrived. The Romans noted that the Britons kept chickens only for fighting and did not eat them. In 1000, chickens, ducks, geese, and pigeons would be found in most villages. Domesticated pigeons were so varied that until Darwin demonstrated that they all descended from the same Indian rock pigeon, the various breeds were thought to be different species.

Lacy and Danzinger praise the pig as the most useful of the English farm animals as nearly every part of a pig can be eaten or used for some purpose, and pigs will eat nearly anything. Bears served a similar purpose for the Indians. "Pannage" or "mast" was what domesticated pigs ate as they made their way through a forest. In addition to its timber, the value of a forest was calculated by how many pigs it could sustain. Other farm animals of the period would appear stunted by modern standards, or Roman standards.

Besides culling the sheep and poultry and fattening off the pigs for butchering in a month's time, September was also the best time of year for the delicate craft of grafting. For centuries, monks had grafted one tree onto another. In time their orchards came to include many varieties of apples and pears, peaches, plums, figs, quince, and mulberry.

Yeomen and their families ate a lot of peas, cabbage, carrots, and onions, which could all be dried or kept in a root cellar, supplemented by greens which grew wild, like purslane or pigweed. Long beans, cauliflower, broccoli, spinach, and beets had not yet been developed. Economics would have dictated a diet of plentiful amounts, in season, of animal protein and fat, with large amounts of vegetables. Bread served as meat when actual meat was scarce and as the source of additional energy needed to complete a day's tasks.

Sugar first arrived in Venice in 996 but did not yet trade as far west as England. It did not become popular until centuries later when slave-powered plantations in the Caribbean made it plentiful and cheap.

Honey was the unparalleled sweetener in 1000, with the pulp of crushed grapes a distant second. Honey was highly valued. It sweetened, it preserved, and it helped heal wounds. Most importantly, it could be converted into mead. The propolis and wax of the hives also had great value. The best candles were made of beeswax. Yeomen made do with smelly ones made of tallow. Bees were a blessing if they nested on your land. Livestock standards had slipped since the time of the Romans, but beekeeping had advanced, and so the vineyards and orchards of 1000 probably surpassed those of the Romans.

By 1000, the Indians of the Eastern Woodlands had been tapping sugar maples for several thousand years. The sap, 10–15 gallons from each tree, was reduced by freezing and boiling to yield about two quarts of syrup. Maple syrup keeps indefinitely. It may have been used as a preservative, but it does not promote wound healing and it cannot be converted into alcohol.

From the beach on Lake Michigan up to what today is Green Bay Road the change in elevation varied with the level of the lake, but it was probably never less than four hundred feet. Green Bay Road follows a ridge, north to south, the high point between the ravines to the east and the land to the west which, while still wooded, was more open with high meadows interspersed with wetlands. Continuing west, the land rises again before leveling off into fields and forest with ponds that beavers created on the small tributaries of the northern branch of the Chicago River. About three miles more to the west of this marshy area, also running north to south, was the Des Plaines River, maybe forty feet across.

In eight miles east to west, the Indians had a beach, an oak forest, meadows, and wetlands with a variety of flora and fauna. A settlement near the lakeshore could have drawn on the largest body of fresh water in the world. Further up the ravines, on the plateaus between them, seeps could have been developed into wells and clearings created for settlements. Two miles west of Green Bay Road, west of what today is Waukegan Road, artifacts found in the archaeological dig conducted in 1991 indicated occupation 1000 years earlier and as much as 9000 years before that.

Baked pumpkin topped with maple syrup and roasted hickory nuts is one Indians in tenth-century Lake Forest might have enjoyed. They may have had excellent food, perhaps fresh herbs with mushrooms sautéed in bear fat with a fillet of fresh-caught lake trout. The recipe may have been worked on for eight thousand years.

Without enough people, existence would have been difficult. One would have to gather both wood and water. There would be no specialization, no saving of time. How many people could have survived in the 21 square miles of Lake Forest and Lake Bluff? Water would not have been a limiting factor, nor material for housing and heating. Breaking the earth, planting a crop, caring for it, harvesting it and preparing it required many calories. If a crop did not at least return the calories it took to grow it, it would have to have some other purpose and be balanced by crops which did return a good surplus. When corn and beans became available, the Indians continued to plant pumpkin and sunflower and Jerusalem artichoke, but they abandoned all the plants with the tiny seeds that they had lived on for the last eight or nine thousand years. The weeds had scarcely been worth the effort.

The Jerusalem artichoke produces tubers which can be harvested from spring until the ground freezes. They are perennial, and they grow easily. They can be baked, steamed, or eaten raw.

However, to do well, they need replanting, and the tubers do not keep very long after being dug up. They can cause severe indigestion, and they do not provide many calories. The seeds of Jerusalem artichoke and the larger ones from the sunflowers can be kept.

Sunflowers were one of the first plants the Indians of North America domesticated. Starting with small plants with multiple flowering seed heads, Indians bred sunflowers with few or singular heads and developed their seeds to nearly a thousand times larger than what they started with. Purple and yellow dyes were derived from the flower, and a black dye from the shells. The seeds, when roasted and boiled, produce a coffee-like beverage. The interior is about ¼ protein, ¼ carbohydrate, and ½ oil.

The Indians in Lake Forest could also have grown a variety of squash and pumpkin whose interior flesh, seed meal, and flowers are all edible. Indians were quick to adopt them when they acquired seeds from the Europeans, but no melons were native to North America.

Storable calories were hard to come by without grain, and those which the Indians could obtain required much more labor than was needed in England. Even in the warmer climate of the period, arrowroot (taro) would not have grown that far north. The plant called arrowhead or Indian cucumber may have been plentiful, but it is low in calories. Cattails would have been plentiful throughout the marshy areas. The entire plant is edible, and parts of it can be harvested eight months of the year. It is rich in carbohydrates. Before the digging of the Skokie Ditch, in the warmer, wetter weather of 1000, when beavers were plentiful, cattails could have been a major part of the Indians' diet. But only its seed and pollen can be stored.

As the Indians prepared for winter, they would have hunted the large birds now returning from the north, or perhaps they paddled to distant rivers to fish and celebrate the bounty of the lake with other tribes congregating on Green Bay and Lake Winnebago.

Bears made their way through the forest and meadows, eating to put on weight for the coming winter and hibernation. Although they are as omnivorous as humans, the population of bears may not have been great. They would have competed with wolves and pumas, and each bear may have required a lot of acreage. Individual bears would have become familiar to the tribe, and their sites of hibernation known early each winter, traced by dogs. Bears were the largest animal living near Lake Forest. A medium-sized bear would yield 70 pounds of meat, but bears need to be butchered and eaten almost on the spot as the meat, so well insulated by its fur, spoils quickly. A similar amount of fat could be consumed or used for other purposes. Though never domesticated, bears might have been selectively harvested with neighboring villages gathered for the feast and to take home their share of the long bones and fat.

October

The Julius Work Calendar's scene for October is of two men hunting with falcons. Again, judging by their fancy dress and their use of falcons, which take forever to train, they too are noblemen.

One of the birds they are hunting is the large European crane, which was extinct by 1600. By 1000, bears were already extinct in England/Scotland/Wales. Reindeer were soon to go. Moose would be gone by the 1300s, beavers in the 1500s, and wolves in the 1700s.

Lacy and Danzinger state that until 1066, when the Normans came to rule, that all men had the right to hunt. Yet, the two men are not dressed like most of the men in the illustrations of the previous months. They wear capes and boots. One of them rides a horse, and both have falcons on their arm. They are not yeomen. Only the men feasting in April, the solitary hunter in August, and the two hunters in September are as well dressed. Most of England's forests had been converted into pasture and farmland. Large game was scarce. The yeomen might be permitted squirrels and hares, but not the deer or the cranes. Killing a deer, even being in possession of an arrowhead made for deer, could get a yeoman hanged.

The yeomen might be required to participate in deer drives as beaters. Their lord and his friends would chase after the deer on horseback and attempt to shoot them with bow and arrow. Six hundred years later, owing to the Columbian Exchange which brought horses to the Americas, Indians on the Great Plains would be doing the same with buffalo.

It was over well before Wounded Knee, but the three hundred years of living as horse people on the endless Great Plains must have been exhilarating. Parkman observed, though, that it was hell for the women and dogs.

Settled now only in winter, the Plains Indians followed the buffalo herds eight months of the year. Moving frequently, sometimes daily, they were often now, because of the horse, much further than before from rivers and streams. It was hard to keep clean after butchering buffalo. There were few trees on the prairie but a lot of sun and wind-blown grit. Parasols would later become major trade items for both men and women.

Dogs of the Great Plains lost much of their status when horses were introduced in the 1500s. For 16,000 years, they had been the only pack animal that the Indians had, and people traveled at a human's walking pace. Now, people traveled at a horse's walking pace, and the poor dogs, dragging their travois, were expected to keep up. Even the most miserable small pony could replace him. He had fallen from man's partner from the time before time to one whose existence depended now on the balance of more pasture vs. the unwanted parts of elk and buffalo. Dogs had always been dispensable, but now, much more so than before.

Still, they tug at our heartstrings.

Eloquence in speech was admired and practiced by the Lakotahs, with whom Francis Parkman spent most of 1846. He records a Lakotah woman as she addressed her dog before clubbing him to death.

"You ought to be ashamed of yourself!"

"I have fed you well, and taken care of you ever since you were small and blind, and could only crawl about and squeal a little, instead of howling as you do now. When you grew old, I said you were a good dog. You were strong and gentle when the load was put on your back, and you never ran among the feet of the horses when we were all traveling together over the prairie. But you had a bad heart! Whenever a rabbit jumped out of the bushes, you were always the first to run after him and lead away all the other dogs behind you. You ought to have known that it was very dangerous to act so. When you had got far out on the prairie, and no one was near to help you, perhaps a wolf would jump out of the ravine; and then what could you do? You would certainly have been killed, for no dog can fight well with a load on his back. Only three days ago, you ran off in that way and turned over the bag of wooden pins with which I used to fasten up the front of the lodge. Look up there, and you will see that it is all flapping open. And now tonight, you have stolen a great piece of fat meat which I was roasting before the fire for my children. I tell you, you have a bad heart, and you must die!"

Overhunting and the destruction of its habitat made the European crane scarce. Its scarcity increased its value which made it ever scarcer until it was gone. This pattern repeated in the 1800s. The great auk, a Northern Hemisphere version of a penguin, once lived from Canada to Greenland to the

Orkney Islands off of Scotland in an arc across the North Atlantic Ocean. By the early 1800s, great auks had become scarce. Newspapers and museums offered rewards for their capture. The competition grew fierce, and the last of the once multitudinous bird was killed in 1844. Sixty years later, the passenger pigeon in North America followed it into extinction. There had been billions.

Lacy and Danzinger propose that the two gentlemen with the falcons are forming or strengthening an alliance. The authors reckon that from 950 to 1066, England was the most fought-over real estate in western Europe. Deer hunting in the fall with yeomen acting as beaters might have served to maintain an alliance but also provide military training.

It was the law in England that every boy who was not a slave, upon reaching his twelfth birthday, "shall swear in the name of the Lord, before whom every holy thing is holy, that they will be faithful to the king." This oath was administered by the local sheriff. It bound the boy to the king. He was now responsible for the loyalty of his family and everyone else in his community.

The local nobleman could be a tyrant. Loyalty and combat proficiency was what made him valued by his king, that and the revenue he could raise. The nobles held their positions at the pleasure of the king. Dismissal often meant death. The squeeze was universal. The push for productivity and taxes and the required manual and military service must at times have pushed the yeoman's life to the edge. 1000 was not the time of chivalry. Even the concept did not exist for several hundred more years.

Every fall, small armies marched and maneuvered under the direction of their nobles, training to or, given an opportunity, seizing adjacent land and its inhabitants. The harvests were in and the granaries full. A successful raid was enriching, while an unsuccessful defense meant losing everything. If not killed or taken slave, a yeoman and his family would be destitute with winter coming on, the long, dark winter of Northern Europe.

The victory of the Normans at Hastings in 1066 was due in part to English fatigue. Only days earlier, Harold's army had fought a fierce battle to drive away Viking raiders from England's northeast coast. Then they needed a forced march of several days to reach Hastings to contain the invading Norman army. Though exhausted, the English held off the Normans for most of the day. Then their leader, Harold, was shot through the throat, and the English lost heart.

Unlike their Norman adversaries, the English did not specialize as spearmen or archers, or as horsemen. The English did not use their horses in combat but only for transport.

William the Conqueror, the Norman leader, invaded in October. In the spring and summer, his soldiers were busy planting and harvesting, and in winter, warfare was too difficult in the cold.

In October in Lake Forest, birds were migrating south. Deer were at their plumpest. Bears were probably saved until they had gone into hibernation. Beavers were abundant. Over 200 million may have lived in what today is the United States and as many more in Canada. Until Europeans arrived, beavers, not humans, shaped the landscape. Their dams and lodges stayed in place for centuries, and the ponds and marshlands which formed behind them. The trade with Europeans that later started for their pelts reduced these wetlands and their populations of migratory birds, aquatic plants, and smaller animals. From the 1600s through the 1800s, as the Indians acquired trade goods in exchange for beaver pelts, they were also destroying their own habitat.

In Europe, for several hundred thousand years, Neanderthals had lived on mammoths and archaic elephants. A Neanderthal man may not have been much to look at, but some say that if given a shave and a haircut and dressed in a business suit, he could walk around lower Manhattan without drawing notice. He stood about 5' 7" and weighed 140 lbs. Over eons, he had evolved into the best mammoth-killing form his species could produce. He is gone now, except as an ancestor. Those whose ancestry is non-sub-Saharan African carry 2–4% Neanderthal DNA. Those whose ancestry is solely sub-Saharan African carry none. No human today could thrust a spear as hard or cover forty yards as quickly. He did not use an atlatl; some say because he was dim and never figured it out.

Possibly, for his last 50,000 years, he had the atlatl but used it only on smaller game as he found it unnecessary with mammoths. He vanished as a separate species when émigré groups started arriving from Africa.

The forebears of the Indians arrived in North America around 16,000 B.C. where they found mammoths and other megafauna. These large animals had lived in North America for several hundred thousand years. They had survived ice ages and great changes in landscape and vegetation. By 12,000 B.C., they were all extinct.

Indians certainly engaged in warfare. Like Otzi, many of the oldest skeletons found in North America have arrow or spearpoints in them. Barlow, an early English explorer who sailed into Chesapeake Bay in the late 1500s, wrote that the Indians used hardened wooden swords and shields as well as warclubs with spikes, spears, and bows and arrows. His account is interesting if suspect. The Indians he encountered, he said, had not previously seen white men but, according to Barlow, they were growing wheat and oats. There is about an 85-year window during which the Indians might have indirectly acquired these grains from the Spanish, if Barlow was not embellishing.

The individuals who contributed to the gene pool of every Indian who came to occupy North and South America may have numbered no more than fifty. These people, not many, brought with them the dog (3 varieties), head lice, and seeds of bottle gourds. They must have been seafarers, moving eastward from the outlet of one stream in Beringia to another, hunting birds, marine animals, fish, and shellfish. Their eastward drift to North America may have been caused by the need to move along after depleting each area's meager resources. All but small parts of the coastline of Beringia were covered by ice. These individuals may not have been all of one group.

Later, the Indians of North America lost over 99% of their land. Yet, they fared better than others when encountering Europeans and their diseases.

About 100 years before the Pilgrims stepped ashore at Plymouth Rock, Spaniards landed on an island off the north coast of South America. They wore armor. They had war dogs. They had lances, swords, crossbows, longbows, and muskets. The Indians had sharpened sticks. It was not a battle. It was a slaughter. The forest of North America was very much the Indians' friend. Even with metal axes and saws, removing the forest took generations. Until then, those who knew the forest held a great advantage.

The Indians' bow and arrow was as accurate as the early muskets, quieter, and could be reloaded more quickly. Still, the musket became the preferred weapon in the 1600s. Armor made of small branches and shields of fire-hardened wood could protect against arrows but not against a musket ball. After an initial defeat at the hands of the French, the Iroquois heavily hunted beaver and traded the pelts to the Dutch for muskets of their own. Then they raided the French settlements repeatedly. Unless guided through the forest by an allied Algonquin or Huron, the French were unable to retaliate.

Without the diseases the Europeans brought with them, how would the Indians of North America have held up against the Europeans? When the Pilgrims arrived off Plymouth Rock in 1620, the Indians might have turned them away if two years earlier, they had not lost as much as 90% of their population.

Other diseases from Europe ran through the tribes of North America in deadly succession. In England, measles was just one of many expected childhood diseases. In the Americas, it was devastating. Death came not just from the disease itself but also from not knowing how to treat it. Quenching the pain and itching by swimming or rolling in snow killed many the disease might have spared.

October in Lake Forest was warmer then, and the harvest still in progress. Pumpkins, squash, and the seeds of the sunflower and Jerusalem artichoke were collected and stored beneath the sleeping platforms in the long houses, the seeds in wicker baskets lined with treated hide. Waterfowl flying south would put down at night in the wetlands west of Green Bay Road and along the Chicago River. It was the season when lake trout and whitefish swam up streams to spawn. Joining other tribes as they netted and speared the fish would have meant a 30-mile journey south or longer ones north to the Milwaukee River or beyond that to Green Bay. The inflow of fish during the spring and fall spawning runs in Green Bay may have been so great that it occasioned a celebration and feast with the tribes of the Confederacy inviting those to their south to join them. Distances covered by tribes in the 1600s on their way to the fish runs at the outlet from Lake Superior were often much greater than that from Lake Forest to Green Bay.

Life in England had complexities not found in Lake Forest. It was the other way around as well. The French were clearly appalled by the customs of the Indians in regard to torture and cannibalism, but the French were not anthropologists. They came for the precious furs, to spread the Gospel, and to keep other European nations out. If there is an understanding of the underlying reasons for the Indians' consumption of others, it is not likely found among the memoirs of the French priests and magistrates but possibly among those of the Metis, descendants of French men and Indian women, who might "translate" the Indian into European.

Prior to the onset of his death by torture, an Iroquois addressed his Huron captors. "My brothers, I am about to die. Do your worst to me. I do not fear torture or death."

Prior to this ceremonial death, the captive had been adopted into a Huron family. He had lived with them for months. He had shared their meals. He asked his hosts how he was to die and agreed that fire was good. This almost participatory ceremony contrasted with the anger the Iroquois demonstrated some years later when they ate the Jesuit, Pere Brebeuf. Brebeuf was tied naked to a stake and burned repeatedly over his entire body. Brebeuf stood erect and prayed in a loud voice for the deliverance of the souls of the Christian Huron prisoners, who would soon share his fate, and directed to hell those who would do them harm. The Iroquois cut off his lips. They tried every means to make Brebeuf cry out, but he would not but continued to pray and to chastise his tormentors as clearly as he could. Although enraged by the priest's steadfast refusal to express suffering, upon his death, the ranking Iroquois chief cut out Brebeuf's heart and consumed it, honoring him. Others ate the rest of Brebeuf. Years later, his skull was recovered. It is now in a silver reliquary at a seminary in Quebec.

Not many years before Brebeuf died, one Francois Ravaillac assassinated the French king, Henry IV. Ravaillac was burned with sulfur, then with boiling oil, and finally with molten lead. His flesh was torn from his body with white-hot iron pincers. Ravaillac was still alive. His limbs were tied to horses and he was slowly pulled to pieces. At this time in England, treason was punished by hanging the man or woman until near death, then tying them to a stake and disemboweling them while keeping them alive, and then finally pulling them apart with horses. Torture was an accepted part of European life. It was more the cannibalism that got to the French priests. At times, as with Brebeuf and other captives, there appears to be a sacramental aspect. At other times it seemed to result from convenience. Rather than fish or hunt for game on their return to their villages with hundreds of Huron captives taken in a raid, each night on their journey home, the Iroquois ate some.

Cannibalism was not restricted to the tribes of the Northeast, and it did not end any time soon after contact with priests or other Europeans. One hundred years later, during the French and Indian War of 1754-1763, which in Europe became the Seven Year War, the French, on several occasions, found it expedient to look the other way when their Indian allies indulged in the practice. Facing the vastly larger number of English troops in North America, the French had recruited Indians from tribes living as far to the west as Iowa and Minnesota. Some traveled nearly 1000 miles to aid in the defense of New France and its principal cities of Montreal and Quebec.

Not willing to risk offending their ferocious, if often feckless, allies, the French let the Indians boil an Englishman and feast on him in the very center of Quebec.

England in 1000 had trade and tariff agreements with city-states in Italy. Trade could not have been as extensive in Lake Forest, and yet, for a path to remain open through a forest, constant use was needed. Pere Marquette and Joliet in 1673 went from Green Bay to Lake Winnebago and from there by portage to the Wisconsin River and the Mississippi. Another route began at the bottom of Lake Michigan, went up the Chicago River, and by portage to the Illinois River and downstream to the Mississippi. Marquette and Joliet took this route on their return. There were few tracts through the interior. The trail, which became Green Bay Road and others which in places ran parallel to it, may have started as game trails.

Buffalo migrated to and from the Great Salt Lick in Kentucky along the same path each year. In some places, they created gullies six feet deep. Deer may have started the path that became Green Bay Road, migrating annually to a salt lick in southern Illinois. It's interesting to think that perhaps the trail was developed earlier by mammoths and mastodons, but the region had been scraped clean by glaciers. It still lay beneath the ice long after the last of the great beasts had vanished.

October was the best month for war in England. It may have been the same in Cahokia and in Green Bay and Lake Winnebago. The Indians in Lake Forest would have had difficulty traveling any great distance to make war, carrying rations of seeds or trying to live off the land as they went. They may have known of Cahokia for ten generations, but over the last fifty years, Cahokia must have loomed ever larger on their consciousness. The growth rate of Cahokia is astonishing. It is thought most or all of the tribes on the upper Mississippi River abandoned their villages and moved to Cahokia. They left behind beliefs, practices, and alliances as well as their dwellings. Now they grew corn, built mounds, and accepted a new god of the sun and its corn. Cahokia put aside surplus in good years to cover the bad and, in this way, could have fed recent migrants from the upper Mississippi who may have suffered draught or a prolonged winter, or who may have come to Cahokia under threat.

In Mexico, where corn was developed, Indians worshiped the sun and practiced human sacrifice. At the top of their tallest mound, that closest to the sun, the Indians at Cahokia may have done the same. Admittance to Cahokia and its food may have come at a cost to desperate tribes: their daughters. It might not have been as dark, but the discovery of buried groups of young women indicates that it may have.

November

The November scene from the Julius Work Calendar is not immediately understood. Three men are well dressed and wearing boots. A fourth is poorly clad and barefoot. In the background, a fifth is carrying a load of lumber on his shoulder. Lacy and Danzinger interpret the scene as showing the barefoot lad and the one walking away with someone else's lumber as one and the same. The thief has been apprehended and brought before the law. He is about to undergo punishment, or rather, a divine inquisition. He must grasp a red-hot length of iron and carry it nine paces before he can let it go. His hands will be treated and stay bandaged for seven days. When the bandages are removed, if the skin is healing, the verdict will be one of not guilty. If his wounds are festering, he will be hanged and left until birds have eaten the flesh from his bones.

Judgment and punishment must have occurred among the Indians of Lake Forest, but their smaller populations would not have allowed for such a hierarchy and, perhaps, not for theft either. Thievery might have been pointless. There were few secrets in an Indian village. The Indians were much less private in all aspects of their lives than the French priests who wished to live among them. The desire of the priests for solitude during prayer caused great mistrust. Desire for privacy drew suspicion, and among a small group, it would be impossible to pass off another's stolen cloak or spear as your own.

What was of value to the Indians was not well understood by Europeans, then or later.

The Indians in Lake Forest may have lived in a manner not too different from an Algonquin tribe in Nova Scotia that the Jesuit, Pere Biard, wrote about in 1614. These Indians practiced no agriculture at all. Biard makes their life sound idyllic: dining on seal early in the year, then beaver, moose, and bear. In April, smelt and herring ran up the streams and waterfowl laid eggs all over the beaches. Summers were easier still with endless amounts of food available. In September, eels swam upstream. Then it was back to beaver and moose. But it was a fragile life, one without much cushion. They might suffer over a harsh winter and lose many of their tribe. These Algonquins had once lived in the territory then occupied by the Iroquois.Now, they lived on its extreme outskirts, and only at the tolerance of the Iroquois who knew that they themselves could not grow corn in such an inhospitable location.

The greatest human carrying capacity for the 21 square miles which constitutes Lake Forest and Lake Bluff was probably reached many times during the several thousand years that preceded European contact. 1000 was warmer; its winter shorter and its growing season longer. The area west of Green Bay Road would have held a great deal more water because of the activity of the beavers over centuries. The Indians created growing areas on patches of higher ground using tree-ringing and fire. Their gardens of seedy plants, pumpkins, and sunflowers could be maintained whether the tribe was down on the beach or over west on the Des Plaines River as the distances were not great.

The Lake Forest tribe's way of life would have been similar to that of the Algonquins on Nova Scotia but different in one important way. They had some crops, some cushion. They would also have had a greater density of population and been more involved in trade.

The Iroquois were a confederacy of five tribes. From east to west along the Finger Lakes region of northwest New York were the Mohawks, the Oneidas, the Onondagas, the Cayucas, and the Senecas. Iroquois villages were not large as each sub-tribe had many. These tribes kept peace with each other. There were quarrels, but they never fought one another. Any of the tribes might decide to wage war on the French. It bound none of the others, and peace with one tribe did not mean peace with the others. Any man could wage war. He merely had to say he was going to war and ask those who would to join him. Even with corn and beans included in their diet, the greatest number of warriors the Iroquois could put into the field in the 1600s was less than 2300.

The confederated tribes I imagine inhabiting Green Bay-Lake Winnebago lived in an area somewhat larger than the Finger Lakes region in upstate New York. From its mouth at the top of Green Bay, the Fox River runs 40 miles up to Lake Winnebago, itself 30 miles in length. Protein and fat from fish, birds, and deer would have been abundant, as would edible greens. Wild rice would also be available for much of the year. This represents a good, perhaps an ideal diet.

Cahokia's rise came about on the abundant calories of corn. At first, the deficiency of the essential amino acid, tryptophan, would be covered by the fish caught on the Mississippi River and the deer brought in from outlying tribes. Increasingly though, as its population grew, Cahokia came to rely disproportionally on corn. Cahokia's end came on like a supernova. After drawing in everything around it, Cahokia collapsed and blew apart, scattering its people to the winds.

Centuries later, white settlers attributed the 200 massive earthen structures to Egyptians, to Assyrians, to Greeks, to Phoenicians, to very nearly anyone not Indian.

December

Lacey and Danzinger don't spend much time discussing the last illustration of the Julius Work Calendar. Two yeomen are using flails, knocking grain from stalks. Another man is sharpening a tool on a grindstone while beside him a fourth man is raking up the stalks already flailed. Two more are carrying away the discarded stalks in a basket they carry between them. These activities all occurred earlier in the year. The drawing represents a clearing out of the old to begin anew.

The authors attempt to reconstruct the mindset of the English in the year 1000, their view of the world, their spirit.

In Revelations: 20: 1–3, John of Patmos writes of the end of 1000 years when "the dragon, that serpent of old, the Devil or Satan, was to be let loose for a short while." Fear was widespread that Satan would soon be among them, according to one manuscript which survives from that era, the account of a monk named Ralph Glaber. During his interesting life, Glaber was expelled from six monasteries. Some have questioned his veracity. Ralph recorded that in 1003, the worst having not occurred, in thankfulness to the merciful God who had protected them, the English restored all their churches. Then, as 1033 approached, it became feared that the 1000-year confinement of Satan began with Christ's death and not his birth. Heresies broke out and famines occurred, even cannibalism, but Glaber also recorded that unprecedented numbers of pilgrims set off for Jerusalem, which must have been expensive journeys. Others traveled about the great cities of Europe to hear well-known debaters duel over questions of philosophy.

Arabic numerals appeared in Europe at this time. 999 was adapted in preference to CMXCIX. Also coming from the East through trade was the abacus. Its use spread widely. It was almost a thousand years before it was improved upon.

Sugar and other spices from the East Indies appeared in Mediterranean markets for the first time. Despite the Vikings, things moved ahead. The Vikings may have helped, opening trade routes from the Baltic through Russia to the Black Sea. Mozzarella cheese was first produced from Indian water buffalo brought to Italy by Vikings. North American furs may have been sold in the markets of Venice and Sicily, competing against those from Siberia.

Vikings occupied Lance au Meadows in Nova Scotia around the year 1000 for about 35 years, abandoned it for a few decades, and then reestablished it for another fifty. After many years, it was realized why the Vikings picked this location: "bog iron." The Vikings recognized the site as similar to ones in Scandinavia where, over eons, iron particles moving downstream became enmeshed in the roots of plants. Lance au Meadows was a foundry. Iron objects recovered included items needed to repair ships for return voyages or to continue southward, further down the coast. Other items found were kettles, pans, axes, and saws, which strongly suggests trade with the Indians. What the

Vikings traded for must have been furs and tall trees for masts and buildings and for wood in general as Greenland had none and Scandinavia was further away. At least some contact with the Indians occurred. Amerindian DNA has turned up in Greenland. If Vikings transmitted Old World diseases to the Indians, they did not pass along smallpox, which is something they did do along their trade routes throughout Europe.

Changes would have been occurring in Lake Forest. Archaeological remains in Cahokia indicate that at that time, the inhabitants of the vast city ate a lot of deer. In particular, they ate disproportionate amounts of the prime cuts. Whole deer and the best parts of others were moving from outlying tribes into Cahokia.

Lake Forest was over 300 miles from Cahokia, further by river. It would have been impractical for Cahokia to impose a tribute of deer on Lake Forest, but they may have demanded tribute in a different form, such as labor on their enormous mounds. These Indians, corn-growers from the south, had chosen Cahokia for its soil. They would not have strip-mined this soil to create the mounds. The dirt for them was brought in, requiring even more labor. Over 200 mounds were built around Cahokia. The largest, Monk's Mound was 25,000,000 cubic feet. The largest earthen structure ever built in Europe, Silbury Hill in England, was half that.

In the 1600s, the Iroquois sent war parties from New York to the western Great Lakes. In 1000, Cahokia, fueled by the same corn, and at such a shorter distance, could easily have imposed its will on Lake Forest.

In the early summer of 1653, the Chippewas and Hurons resolved to attack the Iroquois at their point of entry onto Lake Superior, but they failed to gain the advantage of surprise and had to break off the fight, retreating well away from the Iroquois. Warfare among Indians had traditionally been waged in daytime. That way, a warrior would know that his soul would not wander lost forever, as would happen if he were to die in battle at night. The Iroquois had repeatedly broken that tradition in their warfare against the French, the Hurons, and the Algonquins, but they appear to have expected the terrified Hurons and Chippewas to honor it. That night the Hurons and Chippewas returned. Finding no guards, they slaughtered the Iroquois in their sleep.

This setback did not discourage the Iroquois. They sent out war parties for years. Why they were so driven to make war on their distant neighbors is not known. The population of the five tribes of the Iroquois declined to where, rather than kill captured women and children, the Iroquois adopted them into their tribe to maintain their numbers. As the historian, Francis Parkman, observed, in time, the majority of Iroquois were former captives. Parkman attributed the tribe's decline in population to the constant warfare, and it certainly may have been a large factor.

At the same time though, Parkman also relates that the Jesuits, who recorded their experiences in annual reports ("Relations") to the head of their order in France, wrote of a band of Hurons who blamed the Jesuits wintering with them for an illness that killed half their village. The Hurons may have been correct, that it was the priests who brought in the disease. It is just as likely, though, that the Hurons themselves brought the disease back to their village after picking up the illness from the French traders they interacted with in Montreal.

Every new arrival from Europe was a potential carrier of an illness that, until then, was unknown in the New World. The Iroquois interacted with the Dutch, and with the French in their raids upon them, and now with the diseased Hurons whom they massacred and ate. As disease after disease was brought in by Europeans and then by Africans, the Indian population continually dropped. By 1800, tribes that had been habitual enemies were needing to merge. The Creeks, whom the Americans defeated in 1814 under General Andrew Jackson, included a large number of non-Indians, with many runaway slaves, whites, and people of mixed race. Jackson was of Scotch-Irish extraction. So were the three head chiefs of the Creeks. One may have been 7/8.

There were probably settlements north and south of Lake Forest, running along the north branch of the Chicago River and along the Des Plaines River. Disputes with neighboring tribes would arise. There was a reason for the palisade of stakes. Yet, maintenance of what today is Green Bay Road indicates peace generally existed along its route. To warrant the effort of clearing fallen trees and keeping the path open, the traffic pulled by dog-travois must have been of great value. The primary item could only have been salt.

Every tribe would have needed it for flavoring and nutrition, for curing hides, preserving meat, and baiting game. In the same way that a trail ran from Chicago north through Lake Forest all the way to Green Bay and beyond, one must have run from the Saline Springs in southern Illinois north to Chicago. The trail may have been started by herds of migrating deer and possibly caribou, elk, and buffalo, on their way to and from the salt springs. Later, it was maintained for the passage of travois-laden dogs carrying salt.

These far-traveling traders would also carry other items north on their travois and copper awls, bearberry leaf, and birch bark on their return from the north at the end of each summer. The path would have been traveled by commerce between local villages. We think of the Indians as being constantly at war because the period from first contact with Europeans to Broken Knee was generally one of constant war. However, 1000 may have been peaceful with populations near to what the land could support.

If enough salt moved north, the Indians might have changed migration patterns. The deer may have stopped migrating and come to rely instead on the salt left out for them. While they could not domesticate deer, the Indians may have tempted them into dependence.

1000 was warmer by several degrees than today. An enormous expanse of beaver ponds would have kept the air moist in addition to the effects of Lake Michigan and the general pattern of weather passing first over the Mississippi River on its way to Lake Forest.

The oak forest covering the ravines east of Green Bay Road down to the lake may have been so dense that only lichen and moss could grow on the forest floor rather than browse suitable for deer. This niche may have been filled by the lowland caribou, whose diet of choice is lichen and moss. They may have lived all along this narrow corridor on the shore of Lake Michigan which stretched from Chicago to Green Bay.

White-tailed deer and caribou do not live together. The range of the caribou is limited to that which white-tailed deer cannot tolerate. Whitetail deer carry brain worms. Brain worms do not affect the deer, but caribou or moose grazing in the same area will ingest these worms, and for them, the worms are fatal.

The Indians lacked wool, but buffalo hides with the hair left on are warm in sub-zero temperatures, comfortable to lie on in summer, and were what Parkman used in 1846. Jack Sully, a prominent settler/rustler/politician from the Dakotas, found himself caught in a snowstorm. He wrapped himself in the buffalo blanket he carried on the back of his saddle and survived a night with temperatures below minus 20 degrees F. So did his Lakotah pony which had remained by his side. Male Indians wore buffalo hides as cloaks but did not fashion clothing out of them, which would have been very difficult with bone needles.

Their nudity was probably a matter of economy. Deer hide was relatively scarce. Providing men with clothing may have exceeded the supply and would have required more time on the part of the women. By the 1750s, Indian men had taken to wearing loin clothes, probably made from fabric obtained in trade with Europeans.

Parkman noted that when the Lakotah women prepared buffalo hides for use as tepees, they used only those of the female. After they scraped the hides clean on both sides of any hair or meat, the women worked the brains of the buffalo into the hides to soften them and make them durable.

Deerskin provided the best material for women's clothing and for moccasins, also treated with the animals' brains. Further north, wolverine pelts were valued for face coverings in winter as wolverine fur does not frost.

The killing of a large animal must have resembled a modern-day assembly line with the gutting, removing the pelt, quartering, butchering, saving tendons, long bones, hoofs and skull, treating the pelt, and preserving much of the meat.

The optimal size for a village and the spacing of villages had probably evolved thousands of years earlier. When these limits were exceeded, warfare or starvation followed. Overall, populations probably hovered near the carrying point for most of the nine thousand years that Lake Forest was occupied. Awareness of and interacting with seasonal changes and with neighboring tribes, living primarily on what bounty nature provided, the Indians lacked both the means and a reason to make large changes to their environment. Cahokia was a great exception, one which could never have happened on goosefoot and pigweed.

Twenty-one square miles, the area of Lake Forest and Lake Bluff combined, would be a circle with a diameter of nearly seven miles, about as far as a person could walk over and back in a day, on a path.

A tribe of fifty people on 21 square miles would mean about two and a half people for every square mile, a density nearly 500 times greater than that estimated for the Upper Peninsula of Michigan. It might seem that between caribou, moose, and fish runs that the Upper Peninsula's carrying capacity must have been greater than not even 100 people. However, the difference may have been that stark. Upper Michigan was more heavily wooded. The plants with the small seeds and the pumpkins and sunflowers might never have matured during the shorter growing season, if they even found anywhere to grow.

Could Lake Forest and Lake Bluff have carried even fifty people? Or perhaps a hundred?

Animal protein and fat would have been abundant at different times during the year. The leaves of their many seedy plants were all edible and as nutritious as modern vegetables. Varieties of pumpkins and squash could be harvested from early July late into the fall, and then kept for several months, and their seeds even longer.

The great difference between Lake Forest and an English village like Isham was that where agriculture could support the latter, it could only augment the diet of the former. Indians in Lake Forest did not alter their landscape as greatly. They were less separated from the rest of nature and more tied to its rhythms and variances. Beliefs and attempts to explain the mysteries of existence, of life and of death, were through a different lens than that of their English counterparts.

Corn and the rising power of Cahokia was a violent change in the lives of the Lake Forest tribe. It may have come on slowly, the reach and power of Cahokia. But by 1000, young men from Lake Forest and neighboring villages were leaving to work in Cahokia.

Imagine a young man from his small village upon seeing Cahokia for the first time, the vastness of the great city and the size of the mounds, over a hundred of them, some as high as a ten-story building. It would have devastated his spirit, rendering meaningless all he had known; his legends, myths, his old gods shown powerless before the new one.

Cahokia did not last long, collapsing and abandoned by 1400. By the time the French first paddled opposite Lake Forest in the mid-1650s, the village may also have ceased to exist.

Afterwards

What really happened in Lake Forest after 1000 no one knows. There is nothing to indicate further occupation at the site west of Waukegan Road.

The village may have been depopulated, all its inhabitants forced to move to Cahokia.

Or, despite having been such a good location for nine thousand years, the site near the Chicago River may no longer have served the needs of the tribe and they may have moved. Not long after 1000, corn which matured quickly enough became available and the Indians in northern Illinois and Wisconsin stopped eating the small seeds. They may also have stopped eating cattail and decided to live closer to the planting areas or even a little further to the east where, at the top of a ravine, they had a view of Lake Michigan.

They could have lived there almost until 1800 and left behind plenty of broken pottery and other debris to attest to their having once been there. But then, in 1900, an industrial baron from Chicago, admiring the same view from the top of the ravine, constructed a summer mansion on the site and the artifacts were buried beneath tons of fill which his architect had added to raise the level of the mansion and improve the view toward the lake.

Archaeology is a recent science and not yet truly respected. In the 1800s, it was worse. The invaders from Europe often sought to destroy all evidence of earlier settlement. In Cahokia they cut away many of the mounds.

Lake Forest is not yet two hundred years old. Indians lived on that land for nine thousand years. For almost all that time they lived without corn. For most of that time they also lived without pumpkin or sunflower. They knew how to survive though, and, perhaps, how to live.

Much of England's history was lost when the libraries were burned. In a way that was regrettably similar, much of what the Indians had learned over many thousands of years of intimate observation of plants and animals and the world around them was also lost, swept away beneath the avalanche from Europe.

www.ingramcontent.com/pod-product-compliance
Lightning Source LLC
Chambersburg PA
CBHW071347150726
47997CB00002B/887